MW01609133

The Acquisition Decision

By

Woods Gordon

A member of Arthur Young International

A study carried out on behalf of the
National Association of Accountants
Montvale, New Jersey
and
The Society of Management Accountants of Canada
Hamilton, Ontario, Canada

Published by

National Association of Accountants
10 Paragon Drive, P.O. Box 433, Montvale, N.J. 07645

and

The Society of Management Accountants of Canada
154 Main Street E., Hamilton, Ontario, Canada

Norma Frankel, Editor
Mandel & Wagreich, Inc., Cover
Copyright by National Association of Accountants © 1985
Copyright in Canada by The Society of Management Accountants of Canada © 1985
Canadian ISBN 0-92021225-5
NAA Publication Number 84162
ISBN 0-86641-110-0

Foreword

Presented here are the findings of a study of corporate acquisitions in the United States and Canada. The study was undertaken to help us understand the vital tasks and decisions involved, especially the related managerial information needs.

Commissioned jointly by the Society of Management Accountants of Canada and the National Association of Accountants, the study was conducted by a Woods Gordon research team through interviews of company executives in order to learn how they actually go about making acquisitions. This method of research enabled the researchers to construct a description of the acquisition decision process in a manner compatible with their assignment of interpreting the role—actual and/or prospective—of management accounting.

Throughout this research report an attempt was made to highlight the experience of successful acquirers. We hope that the report will be of interest to those who are or will become active participants in the acquisition decision process—NAA and SMAC members in particular. We also hope that the insights gleaned from the report will serve them well on their way toward being associated with still more successful acquisitions.

This study represents part of the second phase of a continuing business decision research project sponsored jointly by the Society of Management Accountants of Canada and the National Association of Accountants. This second phase of the research project is composed of a set of fact-finding studies, designed to produce descriptive reports on a set of selected decision processes common to manufacturing firms, excluding the lower-level, highly repetitive, and often fully programmed decision processes such as those related to production scheduling and inventory control.

Nine decision processes were selected during the initial phase of the project. Six of the processes have been covered in previous studies: (1) distribution channels decision, (2) lease-purchase decision, (3) make-buy decision, (4) pricing decision, (5) capital expenditure decision, and (6) new-product decision. The remaining two processes after the acquisition decision will be covered in the near future: (1) divestment (product abandonment) decision and (2) manpower planning decision.

One of the main objectives of the overall business decision project is to explore the potential for developing a management accounting system consistent with the actual decision processes and managerial uses of accounting information. This subject area will be addressed directly in the concluding phase of the project.

The report was written by T.W. Marlow, partner, and M.H. Barbarosh, manager of the merger and acquisition services department of Woods Gordon. The report was edited by R.F. Mason, functional director of the department.

Guidance in the preparation of this research report was kindly and generously provided by the Project Committee:

Paul H. Levine (Chairman)
Magnetic Analysis Corporation
Mount Vernon, New York

Dan Armishaw
The Society of Management
  Accountants of Canada
Hamilton, Ontario

Peter W. Kreutzer
Merland Exploration, Ltd.
Calgary, Alberta

Geraldine F. Dominiak
Texas Christian University
Fort Worth, Texas

Frank L. Sbrocchi
Concordia University
St. Lambert, Quebec

The report reflects the views of the researchers and not necessarily those of the cosponsoring organizations or the Project Committee.

Stephen Landekich
Director of Research
National Association of Accountants

Table of Contents

List of Figures

The Acquisition Decision

Chapter 1

Executive Summary

In 1977 the National Association of Accountants (NAA) and the Society of Management Accountants of Canada (SMAC) began a long-term study of how corporate executives make major decisions. Their purpose in undertaking this ambitious study—called the Business Decisions Models Project—was to explore the possibility of developing a management accounting system that would be fully responsive to the way senior managers actually use accounting information to make decisions.

The project began with three background studies on business decisions and management information: *Impediments to the Use of Management Information* (Henry Mintzberg, 1975), *Normative Models in Managerial Decision Making* (Lawrence A. Gordon, Danny Miller, and Henry Mintzberg, 1975), and *Research Methodology in Business Decisions* (John W. Buckley, Marlene H. Buckley, and Hung-Fu Chiang, 1976). *Normative Models in Managerial Decision Making* identified nine kinds of strategic decisions manufacturing company executives must make that require management accounting information. These nine decision models are:

1. New-Product Decision
2. Distribution Channels Decision
3. Acquisition Decision
4. Divestment (Product Abandonment) Decision
5. Capital Expenditure Decision
6. Make-or-Buy Decision
7. Lease-or-Buy Decision
8. Pricing Decision
9. Manpower Planning Decision

With respect to each of the nine decision models, the objective was to reflect the thrust of the normative or "how to" literature by setting out a brief introduction, a flowchart detailing the activities undertaken and the decision points, a narrative description (emphasizing information requirements) of each step in the flowchart, and a bibliography for each model. These normative models were constructed from a review of existing literature and from studies in the field.

The Business Decision Models Project was a normative study that called for follow-up empirical studies to reveal the differences, if any, between the normative literature and actual management practice. The empirical studies were recommended to reveal how decisions actually are made and the kinds of information used in arriving at decisions.

The Acquisition Decision Study

The *Acquisition Decision* study is the seventh of the nine empirical decision model studies released. The previously published decision model studies are:

1. *The Lease-Purchase Decision: How Some Companies Make It* and *The Lease-Purchase Decision* by William L. Ferrara.
2. *The Distribution Channels Decision* by Douglas M. Lambert.
3. *The Make or Buy Decision* by Anthony J. Gambino.
4. *The Pricing Decision* by Lawrence A. Gordon, Robert Cooper, Haim Falk, and Danny Miller.
5. *The Capital Expenditure Decision* by Arthur V. Corr.
6. *The New-Product Decision* by Dale and Tonya Flesher and Gerald Skelley.

The Woods Gordon study of acquisition decisions began in March 1980, and all interviews were completed by November 1982. The study's objective was to determine how Canadian and United States senior managers actually go about making acquisition decisions.

The type of acquisitions principally dealt with in the interviews and study were "friendly" transactions involving the purchase of assets or shares of private or public companies with dominant shareholders. We chose to emphasize these kinds of acquisitions because they usually are initiated and consummated by the acquirer's management and generally involve full-scale studies of the companies being acquired. These kinds of acquisitions can be distinguished from takeovers of widely held public companies, where sanguine planning and swiftness of action often win the day, and from so-called "white knight" mergers between public companies designed to fend off unfriendly purchasers, where timing precludes in-depth analysis. We decided not to emphasize these latter kinds of acquisitions because they are usually decided upon under highly variable circumstances.

Throughout our research we attempted to uncover both subtle differences and significant differences in the acquisition process followed by successful acquirers. We also sought to uncover the critical factors affecting the acquisition decision.

Summary of Findings

From the interviews conducted and responses obtained we arrived at four general conclusions and observations, which we set out in Chapter 3. These four general conclusions and observations are supported by our specific findings, which also are set out and discussed in Chapter 3. We found that the chief executive officer's (CEO) commitment to and involvement in the acquisition process was of overriding significance to a company's being a successful acquirer.

The specific findings are related to the various stages in the acquisition process (outlined under "Scope of the Study" in Chapter 2). Each finding is set out separately under the various stages and is followed by a fuller discussion of that finding. Readers may thus focus on the findings of most interest to them. Many of the findings in Chapter 3 represent what we consider to be the critical factors that make a company a successful acquirer. For readers who seek a greater understanding of the nature of the responses to the specific questions raised in the interviews, we have set out in Appendix B the essence of the discussions that took place and the nature of the responses to each question. Appendix B also contains a fuller discussion of the responses and observations included in Chapter 3 because they were not considered critical to a company's being a successful acquirer.

From the empirical research conducted we determined that although the acquisition decision-making process may be similar in all the companies interviewed, each company had an approach to acquisitions that was unique to its management style, organizational structure, and corporate culture. To assist readers in obtaining an understanding of what the acquisition decision-making process could look like in a flowchart, we have shown two flowchart examples of empirical models in Chapter 4. This chapter also includes a comparison of these empirical models to the normative model. We found that the normative model captured accurately the tasks involved in the acquisition process, but it did not provide insight into the approach companies take to making decisions or into how they organize themselves to carry out this process. We hope this study will provide such insight.

Potential Contributions of this Study

This research study offers insight into how major United States and Canadian industrial corporations actually make acquisitions. It provides NAA and SMAC members, who are primarily people with a financial and management accounting orientation, with a discussion of the current practice and approach used in making acquisition decisions.

Throughout the research we sought to collect information on specific phases of the acquisition process to provide insight for inexperienced acquirers on how to be a "successful acquirer." We hope that the description and discussion of how experienced acquirers make decisions and approach acquisitions will help those about to implement an acquisition program for the first time. Further, this research also may help others to modify and improve their existing acquisition programs.

Finally, we hope this study will dispel some of the mystery often associated with how acquisitions are made and give those about to embark on acquisitions the confidence that comes with understanding the approach used by experienced practitioners of the art.

Chapter 2

Research

Methodology

Throughout this study we have used certain terms in very specific ways. These terms are defined below:

- *Acquisition*—includes all methods of achieving a combination of businesses under common control, usually by the direct purchase of assets, by the acquisition of control of a business by purchasing the shares of a corporation, or by the legal merger of two corporations.
- *Acquisition department*—refers to a full-time acquisition department staffed with individuals qualified to carry out much of the detailed work required in an acquisition program. This department usually is headed by a vice president of corporate development.
- *Acquisition process*—refers to the tasks a company must undertake, the decisions it must make, and the way it organizes itself to perform the tasks that make the decisions that lead to the purchase of all or part of the assets of another business. Describing this process is the principal focus of the study.
- *Acquisition program*—refers to those stages in the acquisition process that follow a decision actively to seek acquisitions but precede the negotiation of a final agreement of offer and sale. These stages frequently require a high level of support from the full-time staff of an acquisition department, where one exists.
- *Acquisition team*—as used in this report, those people involved in the entire acquisition process, other than the board of directors. It includes the CEO and his senior vice presidents,

as well as the support staff used to carry out specific tasks throughout the process.

- *Broad acquisition criteria*—criteria established to make the initial identification of potential acquisition candidates.
- *Corporate group*—the CEO and those of his senior vice presidents who are members of the acquisition team.
- *Detailed acquisition criteria*—very specific criteria, frequently of a financial nature, that are applied in addition to the broad criteria to determine whether a final decision to acquire will be made.
- *Successful acquirer*—We did not try to assess whether any particular acquisition turned out to be a good business decision. We focused on companies that decided to acquire a particular business and were able to do so. Therefore, a successful acquirer is a company that, having decided to expand by acquisition, has been able to consummate a number of targeted transactions. It could easily be suggested that any acquirer willing to pay the price would be successful by our definition. However, as our study demonstrates, price need not be the deciding factor in achieving acquisitions. Although it is important, we found that the way companies and their senior executives approach possible acquisitions and organize themselves to carry out the tasks and make the decisions are more critical determinants of success. Further, the companies in our interview sample were large and financially successful. These organizations generally considered themselves to be sophisticated acquirers who have made good business decisions in the majority of transactions they have consummated.

The Normative Model

The normative model outlined by Gordon, Miller, and Mintzberg in *Normative Models in Managerial Decision Making* is included in Appendix A. In Chapter 4 we compare this model, which is based on a review of published literature in this subject area, with our findings, as illustrated in the empirical models developed from these findings.

Scope of the Study

We have structured the study to address the major areas dealt with in the normative literature as set out in the Gordon, Miller, and

Mintzberg normative model. Thus we addressed these major areas of the acquisition process in preparing the questionnaires that guided our interviews with senior executives. The study showed that the major stages of the acquisition process followed in practice paralleled the stages outlined in the normative model:

1. Definition of corporate objectives
2. Formulation of corporate strategy
3. Development of acquisition criteria
4. Setting up of an acquisition team
5. Financing of an acquisition
6. Search for acquisition candidates
7. Evaluation of acquisition candidates
8. Consummation of the acquisition
9. Assimilation of the acquired business
10. Conducting of a postacquisition review

Our findings are discussed in the body of the report under these main areas of the acquisition process.

In the course of our interviews we also asked about acquisitions in foreign jurisdictions to determine whether a different approach might be necessary and covered the area of unsolicited and hostile takeovers to ascertain general attitudes to acquisitions under these circumstances.

Approach to Interview Candidates

To obtain as direct a response as possible from the key decision makers involved in making acquisitions, we decided to interview CEOs, vice presidents of finance, and vice presidents of corporate development face-to-face rather than mailing questionnaires or conducting telephone surveys. To increase our chances of reaching these senior officers, we sent our initial request to the CEO. Vice presidents of finance and corporate development are more likely to agree to a request delegated to them by the CEO than to one received directly.

We had originally hoped to arrange separate interviews with each of the CEOs and vice presidents of finance and corporate development of each of the companies we selected. Time constraints, however, forced many of the companies to limit their participation to one senior officer. Thus we had to consolidate our questionnaires into one that included the questions intended for all three senior officers. We believe the study results did not suffer; in many instances the executive being interviewed had held one or more of the other senior positions so that, in fact, all the relevant subject matter was covered in one interview. This situation was particularly true for CEOs, many of whom had previously held one or both of the vice presidential positions.

We have included the consolidated questionnaire, the summarized responses to the questions posed, and the discussion thereof in Appendix B.

Testing the Questionnaires

Having decided to conduct face-to-face interviews, we prepared our questionnaire to provide a framework that would channel a relatively free-flowing discussion and eliminate the possibility that major areas of the acquisition process would be missed. The questionnaire generally avoided questions that demanded yes or no responses.

We tested all our interview questionnaires—one for the CEO, one for the vice president of finance, one for the vice president of corporate development—by holding interviews with someone in each of these positions. These tests allowed us to modify the questionnaire to promote free-flowing dialogue covering all the salient areas of interest. We also pretested the consolidated questionnaire with a CEO to ensure that full advantage would be taken of interview time.

The Interview Process

Interviews lasted about an hour and a half. We began by:

- Explaining the nature of the project
- Assuring the executives that their responses would be kept in strictest confidence
- Reviewing the general topic areas, noting that they ranged from the very general—setting corporate objectives—to the specific—methods of financing

As we proceeded from one topic area to the next, we described the types of questions we wanted addressed in each topic area. The executive then spoke extemporaneously on the particular topic area. The questionnaire contained 59 different questions under 11 topic areas.

Our principal objective in each interview was to understand the company's acquisition process. If time required us to omit questions, we chose to omit those seeking greater detail on specific tasks in favor of more general questions on the decision-making process.

We noted that once an executive began describing how his company went about making acquisitions, he would jump from one topic to another. We encouraged this free-flowing discussion and had no difficulty in capturing responses to the various questions by following the comments from one topic area to another. Where necessary we would frequently redirect the executive to cover areas that had not been dealt with. While this meant that we were not always able to obtain responses to every question from every executive, we found it an acceptable trade-off for the spontaneity the interviews achieved and the practical observations on the factors and forces that shape real acquisition decisions.

The Sample

Companies Selected

We developed a sample of companies to be interviewed from the Fortune 500 List of Industrials in the United States and the Financial Post 100 List of Industrials in Canada. The companies represented a cross section in terms of sales, assets, and acquisition activity in the five-year period ended December 31, 1981. We based our selection on the following criteria:

- A history of undertaking acquisitions within the last five years
- Corporate headquarters located in the eastern region of the United States and Canada (because of time and cost constraints).

Twenty-nine of the 65 companies approached agreed to an interview with at least one senior executive actively involved in acquisitions. Figure 1 profiles the companies interviewed.

As shown in Figure 1, all the companies in our study were much larger industrial organizations than most private companies. However, the sample did not concentrate on the largest companies in the Fortune 500 or Financial Post 100. Of those interviewed, 70% had total equity of less than $1 billion; 80% had total assets of less than $4 billion, and 62% had total revenue of less than $2.5 billion.

Figure 1 shows the amount of acquisition activity of each of the

Figure 1

SUMMARY OF COMPANY CHARACTERISTICS
(BILLIONS OF U.S. DOLLARS)

Company	Total Revenue 1981			Total Assets 1981			Net Assets 1981			Number of Acquisitions in the Past Five Years, to Dec. 31, 1981		
	<$2.5	$2.5–$6.0	$6.0–$9.0	<$4.0	$4.0–$8.0	$8.0–$12.0	<$1.0	$1.0–$2.0	$2.0–$3.0	<9	9–17	18–25
1	×			×			×			×		
2		×		×				×		×		
3	×			×			×			×		
4	×			×			×				×	
5		×			×			×		×		
6		×		×			×				×	
7			×			×			×			×
8	×			×			×			×		
9		×		×				×		×		
10	×			×			×				×	
11	×			×			×			×		
12	×			×			×			×		
13		×		×			×			×		
14	×				×			×		×		
15	×			×			×				×	
16	×			×			×			×		
17	×			×			×			×		
18	×			×			×				×	
19	×			×			×			×		
20	×			×			×			×		
21		×		×				×			×	
22		×			×			×		×		
23			×	×			×			×		
24	×			×			×			×		
25	×			×			×			×		
26		×		×			×				×	
27	×			×			×			×		
28	×			×			×			×		
29	×			×				×		×		
	19	8	2	25	3	1	21	7	1	21	7	1

companies over five years. We found that although some acquisitions were completed in just a few months, most took six months to two years. Based on this knowledge, we decided that any company completing an average of five acquisitions could be considered an active acquirer, particularly if it viewed itself as active and was continually searching for new investment opportunities. Statistically, 72% of the companies we interviewed had completed less than nine acquisitions and 24% nine to 17 acquisitions in the five years under consideration.

Figure 2 sets out the number of companies interviewed in each state or province. Twenty of the companies were located in the United States and nine in Canada.

Figure 2   LOCATION OF COMPANIES INTERVIEWED

Location	Number of Companies Interviewed
United States	
Florida	2
Massachusetts	2
New York	12
Pennsylvania	4
	20
Canada	
Ontario	8
Quebec	1
	9
	29

We categorized the companies as indicated below to see if there were any correlations between the nature of the company and its approach to the acquisition decision process. We found no direct correlation although we did note some minor differences, which are described in this report.

Nature of Company	Number of Companies	% of Companies
Nondiversified companies (those expanding existing lines of business)	15	52
Diversified companies (those adding new lines of business)	7	24
Conglomerates (frequently holding companies)	4	14
Highly regulated companies	3	10
	29	100

Executives Interviewed

We interviewed 38 executives in 29 companies. Twenty-two companies granting interviews limited their involvement to one senior executive; seven allowed us to interview more than one. CEOs were highly represented.

Position	Number of Officers Interviewed	% of Companies Interviewed
Chief Executive Officer	19	66
Vice President of Corporate Development	12	41
Vice President of Finance	7	24
	38	

Limitations

Because all the people interviewed were senior executives of large corporations, we generally limited our interviews to a maximum of two hours. This schedule gave us enough time to grasp the essentials of the acquisition decision-making process in each of the companies, but it was not enough to permit exhaustive analysis.

The survey participants were not randomly selected, and the nature of the questioning process was not highly structured. However, we found no indication that either a broader or a more random sample of sophisticated acquirers might have produced a different result. In selecting survey participants, we principally considered companies with head offices on the eastern seaboard of North America because of time and cost constraints. Although we did not include total regional representation in the study, we found no indication from our interviews that the results would have been different if we had expanded the companies to be interviewed to include a wider geographic representation.

Chapter 3

Findings and Conclusions

All the individuals interviewed were extremely enthusiastic and cooperative. Some were so interested in the subject that our interviews exceeded the two-hour limit to which we had agreed as a precondition of the interview.

We began interviews by outlining the types of questions we thought might be covered under the general area of setting corporate objectives. The executive's typical response was to explain his relationship with his CEO or, if he was the CEO, to explain his background and general business approach. These discussions provided background on how the particular company's acquisition decision-making process evolved and operated in the context of the general philosophic approach the company had developed toward carrying on its business.

General Conclusions and Observations

The executives' responses led us to these general conclusions:

1. Each company has an approach to acquisitions that is unique to its management style, organizational structure, and corporate culture. However, all the companies followed a similar pattern in making acquisitions and undertook activities as reflected in the normative model.

2. The acquisition process is a combination of the activities and decisions that must be made at each stage of the process. The acquisition decision is not one decision, but a series of decisions made during a lengthy and somewhat complicated process.

3. The hallmark of successful acquirers is their ability to make

all the decisions required throughout the acquisition process on a timely and effective basis.

4. The principal determinant of whether companies were able to make the required decisions on a timely and effective basis was the CEO. His role as a driving force in making acquisitions was essential to:
    (a) create a sense of purpose and direction and
    (b) obtain a commitment from those involved to complete desired acquisitions.

We observed that this sense of corporate purpose and direction and the resulting commitments of those involved in the acquisition decision enabled these companies to overcome the numerous difficulties that normally arise and to do so without losing the momentum required to conclude a transaction. These general conclusions and observations are summarized graphically in Figure 3.

Specific Conclusions and Observations

In arriving at the general conclusions and observations described above, we analyzed the acquisition process with respect to both the specific tasks and the decisions required. Tasks included specific work undertaken; decisions included making a judgment and taking action.

Texts on acquisitions frequently emphasize the tasks undertaken and can leave the reader with the impression that the key to being a successful acquirer is simply to complete the tasks in a logical sequence. We observed that although individual tasks (summarized in Figure 4) are important, the decisions and the approach taken to making them are most critical to successful acquisition programs. Decisions are required both during and upon completion of each individual task. The acquisition process is a combination of tasks and decisions, as reflected in Figure 5.

Making Decisions

We discovered that a successful acquisition program depends on the commitment and involvement of the CEO. When the CEO is actively involved, decisions are made on time and transactions are completed. Without the CEO's involvement, the acquisition process

Figure 3
GENERAL OBSERVATIONS AND CONCLUSIONS

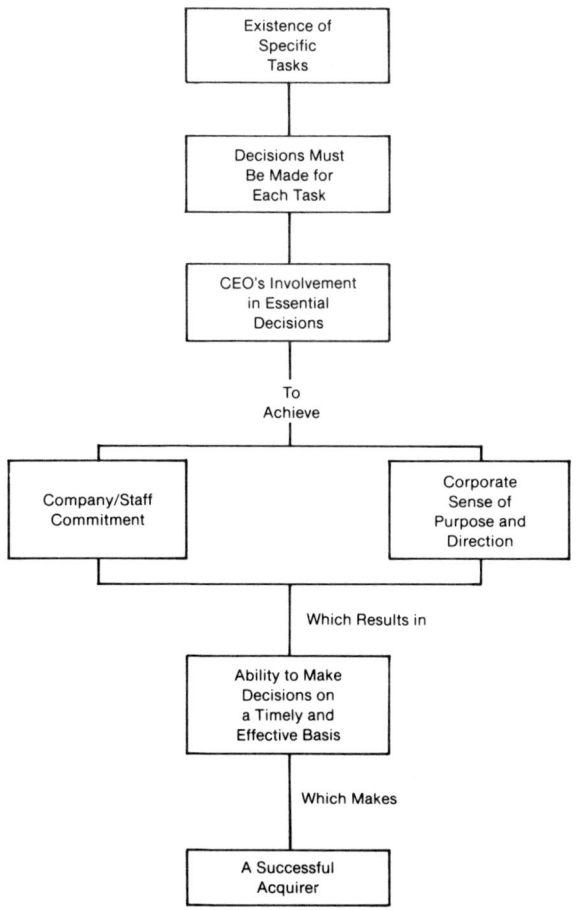

Figure 4
ACQUISITION DECISION PROCESS TASKS

TASKS

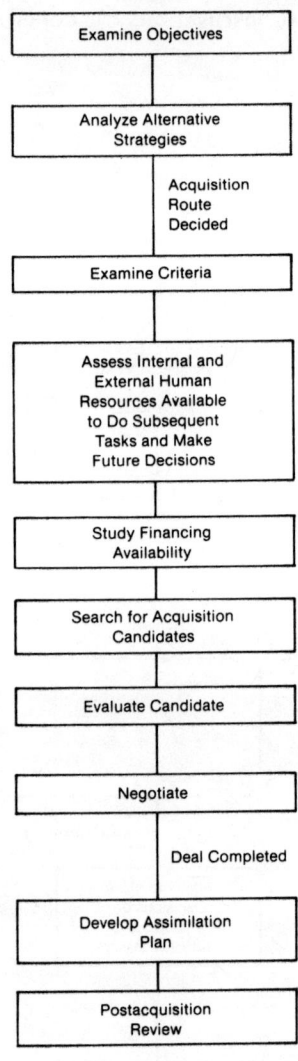

Examine Objectives

Analyze Alternative
Strategies

Acquisition
Route
Decided

Examine Criteria

Assess Internal and
External Human
Resources Available
to Do Subsequent
Tasks and Make
Future Decisions

Study Financing
Availability

Search for Acquisition
Candidates

Evaluate Candidate

Negotiate

Deal Completed

Develop Assimilation
Plan

Postacquisition
Review

Figure 5

ACQUISITION PROCESS TASKS AND DECISIONS

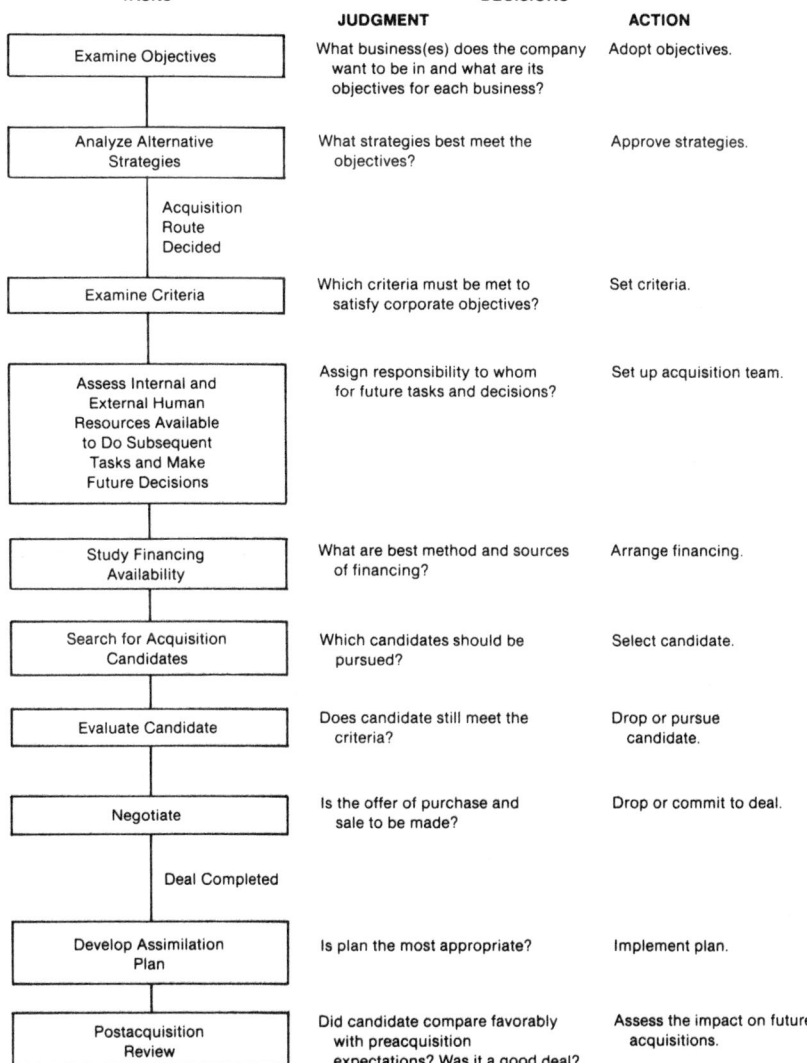

TASKS	DECISIONS	
	JUDGMENT	**ACTION**
Examine Objectives	What business(es) does the company want to be in and what are its objectives for each business?	Adopt objectives.
Analyze Alternative Strategies	What strategies best meet the objectives?	Approve strategies.
Acquisition Route Decided		
Examine Criteria	Which criteria must be met to satisfy corporate objectives?	Set criteria.
Assess Internal and External Human Resources Available to Do Subsequent Tasks and Make Future Decisions	Assign responsibility to whom for future tasks and decisions?	Set up acquisition team.
Study Financing Availability	What are best method and sources of financing?	Arrange financing.
Search for Acquisition Candidates	Which candidates should be pursued?	Select candidate.
Evaluate Candidate	Does candidate still meet the criteria?	Drop or pursue candidate.
Negotiate	Is the offer of purchase and sale to be made?	Drop or commit to deal.
Deal Completed		
Develop Assimilation Plan	Is plan the most appropriate?	Implement plan.
Postacquisition Review	Did candidate compare favorably with preacquisition expectations? Was it a good deal?	Assess the impact on future acquisitions.

can become a meaningless exercise. The desire and commitment of the CEO to make acquisitions appear to have a direct impact on the company's ability to transact. In the companies we interviewed, if the CEO was not a full-time active member of the acquisition team, he maintained close contact with the head of that team and was involved in all critical decisions.

We found, for example, that as a result of this involvement those responsible for making decisions were very confident about the attractiveness of a particular acquisition prospect to the company. This attitude, in turn, allowed them to maintain the momentum and sense of urgency that appeared to be critical for consummating transactions with vendors.

These factors also affect the acquisition process:

- The personality and management style of the CEO
- The reasons for undertaking an acquisition
- The acquirer's corporate structure

CEO's Personality and Management Style

The management style and personality of the CEO usually reflect the corporate culture of the organization and affect the acquisition process. This was particularly evident in the case of authoritarian CEOs, whose direct involvement appeared vital if acquisitions were to be made.

Delegation of the acquisition process by the CEO does not mean that the acquisition process will be unsuccessful. Some CEOs are comfortable with delegating many of the decisions required in the acquisition process. When such delegation indicates a lack of direction or commitment by the CEO to the goal of making acquisitions, however, a successful acquisition program is unlikely.

Because the guidance and direction of the CEO are important to the success of the acquisition process, the CEO's personality will have a great influence on the process. The following personality traits had the most effect:

- *Charisma* and ability to develop a relationship with the prospect. We found this ability to be a strong determinant in the likelihood of completing a deal.
- *Attitude* toward acquisitions. Where the CEO enjoys making acquisitions for his company, the time to complete an acquisition may be accelerated because of his close involvement in the process.

- *Salesmanship.* Where the CEO is capable of convincing acquisition candidates of his sincerity and is able to rationalize the benefits of sale to his company rather than another, deals are transacted.

Reasons for Acquisitions

The reasons for undertaking an acquisition can affect the acquisition process. For example, a high technology company that wants to enter a new market or increase its technology base may have little interest in analyzing the acquisition candidate's financial data. It would be ready to pay the price to acquire the candidate's intangible assets. If, however, the acquirer is interested in a solid cash flow, it will conduct extensive financial analyses to ensure that rates of return are what it would expect from a going concern.

The reason for making an acquisition may also determine how long it takes to do it. For example, if a company is being bought to expand market share and the purchaser is totally familiar with the industry in which the company to be acquired is operating, the purchase price may be determined principally by reference to the known benefits to the purchaser resulting from increased volumes and markets. In such a case, a firm offer may be made very quickly. However, if a company is on the acquisition path in order to diversify and the prospective acquisition candidate is in an industry with which the acquirer is not fully familiar, a very detailed review may be made that will increase the time to complete the deal.

Acquirer's Corporate Structure

The acquirer's corporate structure—particularly whether it is highly structured or less formally structured—also affects the acquisition process. Less structured companies use the corporate group, composed of the CEO and his senior executives, for reviewing acquisitions. Highly structured organizations frequently have a full-time acquisition department. Where such a department exists, the corporate group delegates many of the tasks to be performed in the acquisition process to this department.

We found that in a highly structured company with a full-time acquisition department, it is critical to prevent the more formal reporting relationships from delaying the process unduly if the company is to be a successful acquirer.

We also observed that in addition to the ability to implement an appropriate decision-making process, integral to that process for successful acquirers is an atmosphere of good faith and understanding that has been created among the senior executives in the corporate group. Within this atmosphere everyone acts as a well-coordinated team and speaks with a consistent voice for the corporation when dealing with acquisitions. Where a separate and distinct acquisition department has been established, this sense of commitment and direction is transferred by the corporate group to all the people in that department.

The ability to establish such a relationship appeared to rest principally with the CEO. No matter what the corporate structure, if this internal unity exists, a common sense of purpose between the acquisition candidate and the acquirer also is more likely, and negotiations are facilitated.

When the acquirer acts in good faith and is committed to a deal, a sense of mutual trust is established and information on the candidate's business and operations is supplied more readily. Similarly, when both parties negotiate in good faith and seek to arrive at an equitable outcome for all, the closing of the deal is easier and faster. Furthermore, once the acquirer has established a reputation in the community for being fair, more opportunities are presented voluntarily, mostly, we believe, because companies that want to sell are confident that they will be treated equitably.

Stages of Acquisition

The conclusions and observations described above are reflected throughout the various stages of the acquisition process. Our specific findings on the various stages are summarized throughout the rest of the chapter.

In the normative literature on acquisitions, the terms "objectives," "strategies," and "tactics" are used often but are not consistently defined. For purposes of this report, "objectives" are the goals of the corporation and "strategies" are the specific plans for achieving the objectives. The reader of this study will appreciate that for most of the companies we interviewed, making acquisitions was a principal strategy for achieving corporate objectives. "Tactics" here refers to the manner in which the strategy (in this case, acquisitions) is implemented, which is the essence of this report.

Definition of Corporate Objectives

Finding
   Successful acquirers have clearly articulated their corporate objectives.

Discussion
   Clearly defined corporate objectives appear to be a prerequisite to successful acquisition programs. The emphasis must be not only to define objectives, but also to make sure that they are clearly understood by all senior executives, staff, and outside consultants who will be involved in the implementation of the acquisition program.
   We found that the combination of setting clearly defined objectives and of communicating those objectives to the people involved in the acquisition process was necessary to create a clear sense of purpose. This sense of purpose appears to be common to successful acquirers.

Finding
   The CEO is most responsible for setting corporate objectives, having them approved, and communicating these objectives to others in the organization.

Discussion
   It was evident that when acquisition programs were successful, the CEO was instrumental in that success. He was the motivating and driving force. His initial responsibility for setting the objectives, having them approved by the board of directors, and communicating them to all those to be involved in the acquisition process appeared to be critical to a successful acquisition. A company would be unlikely to become a successful acquirer without this kind of leadership.

Finding
   Most of the successful acquirers did not change their corporate objectives frequently.

Discussion
   It appeared that prior to becoming active acquirers, most of the

companies had devoted considerable time and effort to defining
their objectives clearly. In a number of cases a new CEO had been
hired for the principal purpose of redefining the company's objectives, and this redefinition had led to the company becoming an
active acquirer. However, it appeared that once having set well-
defined objectives, most of the successful acquirers interviewed had
not in any material way changed their objectives. After the objectives were set, the emphasis changed to communicating these objectives to employees and outsiders who would be instrumental in
helping the company reach them.

Formulation of Corporate Strategies

Finding

*Corporate strategies were formulated at the most senior manage-
ment level, with overall approval given by the CEO. The CEO
appeared to be particularly active in setting the strategic plan,
especially where the decision was made to use acquisitions as part
of that plan.*

Discussion

The CEO typically involved his most senior executives in the
formulation of overall corporate strategies, but their degree of
involvement appeared to depend on the CEO's management style.
Where this style was open and participatory, the senior executives
were significantly involved in planning the strategies to be used.

It appeared that the close involvement of the CEO in the process
of developing corporate strategies allowed the senior executives to
become intimately familiar with the CEO's views of the company's
corporate objectives. The communication developed during the
course of establishing agreed-upon corporate strategies was, as
indicated in the discussion of corporate objectives, a critical part of
the acquisition process. This process allowed the senior executives
to get "in tune" with the CEO's personal view of what he wanted for
the company. In all cases the corporate strategies to be adopted were
approved by the CEO. When one of those strategies was acquisitions,
that usually also was approved by the board of directors.

Finding

Although most companies did not make their corporate strate-

gies known publicly, where acquisitions were part of their strategy every effort was made to let it be known that they were in the market for properties.

Discussion

Successful acquirers did not hide their interest in making acquisitions. The CEO, senior executives, and members of the board of directors were all active in maintaining a wide range of contacts and made certain that these contacts were aware of the company's acquisition interests. These contacts included investment banking and business brokerage firms, publishers of acquisition and divestiture newsletters, and the financial press in general.

Successful acquirers, having established a track record, benefited greatly from the business community's awareness of their past success, which appeared to increase the number of acquisition opportunities voluntarily presented to them.

Development of Acquisition Criteria

Finding

Most successful acquirers had both broadly defined and narrowly defined acquisition criteria that they used to assess acquisition candidates.

Discussion

We expect that this approach to setting acquisition criteria may be significant to being a successful acquirer. The broad criteria, though precise enough to allow a quick identification of opportunities to be pursued (and, possibly of more importance, those not to be pursued) were not so narrow as to eliminate most opportunities. The broad criteria seemed to be realistic and were designed to recognize that in the real world the "perfect acquisition" probably does not exist. These criteria could be characterized as either objective or subjective in nature.

Examples of objective broad criteria mentioned in the interviews are:

1. That the company is in a particular industry.
2. That 100% of the company can be acquired.
3. That the business is within a predetermined geographic area.

4. That the company is profitable (e.g., the acquirer will not consider a turnaround situation).

5. That the company has good management willing to stay.

Examples of more subjective broad criteria that were highlighted are:

1. That the acquisition candidate will create hidden value (i.e., the combination of the two entities will produce a value greater than the sum of their individual values: 1 + 1 = 3).

2. That the acquirer's strengths will complement the candidate's weaknesses (e.g., the acquirer can provide access to established distribution networks).

3. That there is a strong advocate within the company for the acquisition. (Some companies would not consider an acquisition unless they were sure that there was someone in the company to run it who would take responsibility for its success or failure.)

4. That the acquisition candidate has the potential of a "hidden oil well" (e.g., the foreseeable introduction of new technology might enhance considerably the value of the assets that are being acquired).

Detailed criteria tended to be more of a financial nature and were applied in the more in-depth reviews of candidates after they had been identified as potential acquisitions. For example:

1. That the investment must produce a minimum stated return on capital employed.

2. That the company must have a minimum stated return on gross sales.

Finding

The prospective acquirer must determine early in the acquisition process whether a candidate is truly for sale.

Discussion

Prospective acquirers do not waste their time on companies that only entertain an unreasonably high purchase offer but are not otherwise for sale. Successful acquirers like to determine early in the acquisition review whether or not the candidate is realistically for sale. The fact that a company was for sale was self-evident when the company was represented by a business broker. When the candidate had been identified internally and it was not known if a sale would be considered, it was usual to contact the owners directly or through an intermediary before spending a great deal of time on further analysis.

Setting Up an Acquisition Team

Finding

All those companies interviewed had an acquisition team responsible for carrying out acquisitions. The two main types of acquisition teams may be categorized as follows:

(i) *Corporate Group.* This group is composed of various senior executives, including the CEO. They interact closely and use support staff as necessary.

(ii) *Corporate Group and Acquisition Department.* Under this structure the acquisition department usually is headed by a vice president of corporate development. The vice president has a full-time staff to carry out many of the steps in the acquisition process. The vice president of corporate development reports to and is part of the corporate group.

Discussion

The structuring of the acquisition team ranged from the very informal and ad hoc approach of assembling a team made up of the CEO and his senior executives and using their staff as required to the highly formalized and structured approach wherein a full-time corporate acquisition department is set up and staffed as part of the acquisition process. These two approaches represent the extremes we found in the companies interviewed. Most of the companies had adopted one of the two basic approaches to organization for the purpose of making acquisitions.

Wherever there was no full-time acquisition department and the acquisition team was made up of members from the corporate group, it was evident that the CEO had a high level of personal interest in acquisitions. Under these circumstances the CEO's approach was very much a "hands on" approach that accounted in large measure for the company's success as an acquirer.

Even where there was a full-time acquisition department, the corporate group did not delegate its responsibility for making and participating in the major decisions in the process. These decisions included whether a candidate had the potential to warrant a more detailed review, whether to make an offer and on what basis, and on what terms to negotiate and make the deal.

Finding

In both types of acquisition structure, the team includes functional experts in such areas as marketing, finance, operations, and legal.

Discussion

Before a deal is concluded, a group of functional experts eventually would have to review the acquisition candidate's operations thoroughly to ensure that all aspects of the company to be acquired are considered fully and evaluated. If the team did not have knowledge in a particular area, such expertise would be obtained from outside the company. The nature of this review by the acquisition team is discussed more fully in a later section.

Financing an Acquisition

Finding

Most companies determined the source of financing available for acquisitions early in the process. This usually took place shortly after the decision to look for acquisitions had been made.

Discussion

Most companies did not like to wait until a deal was almost ready to be closed to start to look for appropriate funding. The chief financial officer was principally responsible for arranging for the availability of the necessary funds.

Finding

The preferred method of funding acquisitions appeared to be highly dependent on the economic environment at the date the financing was being put in place.

Discussion

If there were a consistent consideration given by the companies to the method of funding, it relates to the impact on dilution of the company's reported earnings per share. Where the stock market was placing a high premium over book value on a company's shares, there was almost a universal preference for cash.

Search for Acquisition Candidates

Finding

There were two basic approaches to carrying out acquisition searches—"active" or "passive."

Discussion

In a *passive* search program, the company does not search out or seek to identify and contact acquisition candidates; rather, it waits for opportunities to be presented.

Although the passive search approach may appear to limit a company's chance of finding good opportunities, we found that the organization's success related to the number and quality of its contacts. Such contacts included participants in those industries of interest to the company, investment and commercial bankers, and business brokers. This approach is used most widely where the CEO is actively involved in the acquisition process and he and his senior executives have extensive industry contacts.

Where a full-time acquisition department exists, the company normally carries out an *active* search program. It is also possible, however, for a company with a corporate group of senior executives responsible for carrying out acquisitions to undertake an active search program. An active search program is characterized by one or more members of the company taking an organized approach to identifying and analyzing prospective acquisition candidates.

Finding

When an acquisition opportunity is presented voluntarily to a prospective acquirer, the person responsible for carrying out the review of the acquisition candidate differs depending on the company's structure for undertaking acquisitions.

Discussion

Where a full-time staff group, usually an acquisition department, was responsible for the acquisition review, it would review voluntarily presented opportunities. Where a group of senior corporate executives was responsible for acquisition reviews, one of these officers or the CEO would initially review new opportunities. Where senior officers or the CEO conducted an initial review of such candidates to assess if there was any interest in the opportunity, it frequently appeared to take significantly less time to complete the initial review. However, this comment must be qualified; we found that when the head of the acquisition department performed the initial assessment himself he was able to respond quickly to the company's interest and get a decision on whether further review would be warranted.

Finding

The willingness to use outside consultants to search for acquisition candidates varied.

Discussion

Some companies would not consider allowing such a sensitive project to be carried out by third parties, while others saw it to be an inefficient use of management's time. A number of companies said that the increased ease of access to computerized data bases containing extensive corporate information listings made it easier to perform one's own search. However, particularly in the United States, where an investment banker may be used, acquisition candidate searches often are offered as part of an investment banker's complete service, so companies frequently availed themselves of their financial adviser's assistance in identifying acquisition candidates.

Evaluation of Acquisition Candidates

Finding

The acquisition of widely held public companies by way of an unsolicited offer and the acquisition of privately owned companies represented the extremes in the amount of work done and time spent in evaluating acquisition candidates.

Discussion

When a public company is being acquired, extensive information is generally available from public sources, including SEC filings in the United States. In some cases this information base might provide enough data to determine an offering price. When an unsolicited hostile takeover of a public company is being contemplated, no information is available from the company that can be used to perform a detailed evaluation.

The private company represents the other extreme. Access to detailed information from the company and its shareholders is almost always required before a final decision can be made on whether the company is of real interest to the purchaser. An extensive in-depth anaylsis based on this information is almost always conducted on a private company. The focus of our interviews was on the work done in evaluating private company acquisitions.

Finding

There are basically three levels of evaluation made on private company acquisitions.

Discussion

The first level of evaluation uses readily available information against which to apply the company's broad acquisition criteria. The purpose is to determine whether the candidate is a company the acquirer would like to own. Once the initial evaluation is completed, the acquirer typically contacts the owners and makes an assessment as to whether the company is likely to be for sale at a realistic price before proceeding to evaluate the prospect further.

The second level of evaluation is done on the basis of information provided by the company. A more detailed assessment is made by applying both the broad and the detailed criteria to this information to determine whether the company is of real interest to the acquirer. If, on the basis of this assessment, the prospect is of real interest, acquirers at this point frequently try to get the prospect to enter into a nonbinding letter of intent.

The final level of review generally is described as the detailed purchase investigation and is usually an exhaustive analysis of the company and its business for the purpose of formulating a final purchase agreement. The detailed purchase investigation is completed after the signing of the nonbinding letter of intent.

Finding
Most companies liked to establish as early as possible that the acquisition candidate was a realistic possibility.

Discussion
Because of the extensive amount of time and money required to complete an acquisition, every effort was made throughout the acquisition process to determine that the candidate was likely to be for sale at a realistic price. Thus, once the first level of evaluation was completed so that it was determined that the prospect was of interest to the acquirer, it was usual for the acquirer to approach the owners to ascertain that they would be prepared to sell and to find out what their view was as to its value and the approach taken to arriving at their value. If the acquirer did not believe that the vendor's expectations on value were realistic, he would be unlikely to proceed with further evaluation of the prospect even if provided with extensive additional information on the company.

If these initial hurdles on availability and reasonableness of price range were surmounted, many acquirers liked to get to a point as quickly as possible where they could agree on a value range for purposes of signing a nonbinding letter of intent. Many felt that this furthered the process of reaching a commitment from the prospect on the value at which a deal might be made and reduced the risk of making an unproductive investment in a detailed purchase investigation.

Finding
The principal foci of all levels of the evaluation of prospective acquisitions are on:

(i) *Determining that the prospect meets the acquirer's acquisition criteria, and*

(ii) *Establishing a price that will be offered.*

Discussion

All reports prepared by the acquisition team as a result of its reviews of an acquisition candidate are directed at the two foci listed above. Any evidence that would suggest that the prospect no longer met the company's acquisition criteria was communicated to those who had ultimate responsibility for deciding whether the review should be stopped. Such information was identified and communicated quickly so that needless time and expense would not be incurred if there was no prospect of a deal.

These reports also identify all factors that can be used either in establishing the appropriate approach to value or in identifying items that would result in an adjustment to value. These items are flagged to assist the person responsible for finalizing a deal in his negotiations with the vendor.

Finding

The accounting and tax implications of the proposed acquisition are examined thoroughly, frequently with the assistance of the company's auditors and legal counsel.

Discussion

In most cases, the principal thrust of the accounting review appeared to determine the impact that the acquisition would have on reported earnings per share—probably because our interviews were mainly with public companies. The principal thrust of the tax review was to determine how the acquisition could be structured to minimize the tax cost to both the purchaser and the vendor. The sharing of these overall benefits would be negotiated between the parties in the process of setting the price.

Consummating the Acquisition

Finding

Unless the opportunity was a relatively small one for the prospective acquirer, the decision to proceed to the negotiation phase of the acquisition process was normally approved by the CEO and ultimately by the board of directors.

Discussion

Proceeding to the negotiation stage is viewed as an expression of serious interest and requires senior-level approval. Such approval normally is obtained from the CEO. However, where the acquirer's company is decentralized, the subsidiary or divisional-level president may have authority to conduct negotiations for smaller acquisition opportunities, with final approval by the CEO and board of directors.

Finding

The person who conducted negotiations varied. It was usual for negotiations involving a major acquisition to be conducted by the CEO.

Discussion

The decision on who would be the most effective negotiator for the acquirer was frequently made on the basis of who in the organization had the strongest personal relations with the acquisition candidate, provided that the individual was felt to have the requisite negotiating skills. In highly diversified or conglomerate companies, the president of the operating division or subsidiary that would ultimately be responsible for the acquired company frequently conducted the negotiations, calling on corporate-level assistance when required.

Many corporate-level CEOs interviewed felt that it was best if they avoided being directly involved in the negotiation process so that they could be used as the final decision maker for any disputed issues. By not having the corporate-level CEO directly involved in the negotiation process it was easier for him to settle small negotiation problems and keep the process running smoothly. For large acquisitions, however, the corporate-level CEO normally carries on the negotiations, as his absence could offend the CEO of the acquisition candidate.

Finding

The key to successful negotiations was maintaining trust and momentum from the time of initial contact to finalization of the offer of purchase and sale.

Discussion

It was in the area of negotiation skills that successful acquirers seemed to excel. Many of those interviewed gave us "helpful hints" that they thought had been helpful to them in ultimately being able to complete transactions where others had failed. The creation of a sense of trust was important to limit the number of companies with which the acquisition prospect was negotiating. In many cases if sufficient trust was established the acquisition might even be negotiated on an exclusive basis.

Some of the helpful hints given during the interviews that indicate the importance of establishing trust and maintaining momentum were:

1. Do not intimidate the CEO of the acquisition candidate by letting him feel that his authority will diminish greatly in the new organization. Keep the CEO of the acquirer readily accessible to the CEO of the acquisition candidate.
2. Establish a reputation for treating employees of acquired companies well. A reputation for such treatment becomes widely known and can open up greater opportunities to make other acquisitions.
3. Wherever possible try to be the first potential acquirer into negotiations. This improves the chances of consummating the acquisition.
4. Where an entrepreneurial business is being bought, sell the entrepreneur on the idea that all the routine areas he dislikes, usually in the financial and administrative areas, will be removed and handled by the acquirer, leaving the entrepreneur to devote his time to those areas of most interest to him.
5. Have the ability to structure a deal quickly when an opportunity arises.
6. Wherever possible, avoid getting into bidding matches with others.
7. Do not overcomplicate the acquisition process with unnecessary paperwork and delays. Establish and maintain an open relationship between both CEOs during the entire process.
8. Be sensitive to the opinions and feelings of the acquisition candidate. Take a personal approach to the acquisition.

9. Consider using a "creeping acquisition." Build up from the acquisition of a small interest over a number of years to allow the candidate's management to feel comfortable with your acquiring it.

10. Court the acquisition candidate over a number of years before it considers selling so that should it decide to sell you have the best chance of being considered.

11. Try to avoid trivial matters during negotiations.

12. Visit the acquisition candidate as frequently as possible in order to establish a comfortable working relationship.

13. Attempt to leave the impression at all times that the acquisition process is continuing. This is especially important if the main negotiators are not available because of other commitments.

14. Select the best personal approach in dealing with the key people of the acquisition candidate.

Finding

Once negotiations are completed, the CEO and board of directors approve the final terms of the acquisition agreement.

Discussion

Approval by the board of directors was frequently guided by a recommendation from an executive committee of the board, composed of a small group of directors. This committee was capable of giving senior executives an understanding of how the board would view a particular acquisition proposal. Such comfort enabled key executives to act with confidence during the acquisition process. After negotiations were completed, this committee would support management's recommendations when the opportunity was presented to the board.

Finding

When an unsolicited offer is made, board approval is obtained prior to making the offer.

Discussion

Where management has decided that the best approach to a

prospective public acquisition candidate is to make an unsolicited offer, board approval is always obtained before making such an offer. Because of the wide-ranging implications of making an unsolicited offer it is unlikely that such an offer would be made without board approval.

Assimilating the Acquired Business

Finding
  Most companies interviewed considered the planning for assimilation to be part of the acquisition process.

Discussion
  Many companies considered that their plans for assimilating acquisitions were never as well prepared or thought out as they might have been and felt that if they had spent more time preparing for assimilation they could have eliminated many difficulties they had encountered. Most companies also felt that detailed assimilation plans should be undertaken as early as possible in the acquisition process. They recognized that the urgency of negotiations usually resulted in less urgency being placed on the future problems of assimilation.
  The need for assimilation varied directly with the nature of the acquisition, whether the acquirer operated on a centralized or decentralized basis, and whether the company being acquired was to be operated independently with its own management or was to be integrated with an existing business unit of the acquirer. Many centralized companies automatically changed all policies and procedures of the acquired company to parallel their own. In these circumstances there was a strong need for a definitive program to ensure that the assimilation ran smoothly.

Conducting a Postacquisition Review

Finding
  Those interviewed thought that a postacquisition review was part of the acquisition process, but most admitted that such reviews were not always done as well as they should have been.

Discussion

Most companies thought of postacquisition review as something that took place when success or failure of the acquisition could be determined rather than immediately after the deal had been signed.

The topic of postacquisition reviews is a contentious issue in the normative literature, as some authors are of the opinion that this topic has no place in a discussion of the acquisition process. All those interviewed considered a postacquisition review as part of the acquisition process. Comments were made to the effect that such reviews enhance the acquirer's acquisition ability, as the company learns from past mistakes. However, many companies recognized their delinquency in conducting thorough enough reviews.

Acquisitions in Foreign Jurisdictions

Finding

Most companies interviewed had undertaken acquisitions only in North America. Differences between Canada and the United States were said to be few.

Discussion

Those companies concentrating their acquisition interests in North America found few differences in crossing the Canadian/ United States border. They stated that legal and tax specialists knowledgable in the respective foreign jurisdictions had to be hired to ensure that any acquisition ran smoothly. Otherwise we found no major difference in their approach to making acquisitions in either country. United States executives mentioned, however, that they had found the Canadian Foreign Investment Review Agency to be an impediment to expansion into Canada, although most regulatory hurdles usually could be overcome.

A number of companies noted that the North American market was so large they felt no need to expand off the continent.

Finding

Companies that had made acquisitions outside North America indicated that they did not find many differences or particular difficulties. They again mentioned that when making acquisitions in foreign jurisdictions they required greater assistance from legal counsel and accountants familiar with the rules and regulations in the particular country in which the acquisition was to be made.

Discussion

Most companies making acquisitions outside North America did not find many differences in their approach. However, two caveats noted in foreign acquisitions were the repatriation of earnings and currency fluctuations. Because of repatriation of earnings problems, companies sometimes make acquisitions to use funds that could not otherwise be repatriated.

Hostile Takeovers and Unsolicited Offers

Finding

The use of hostile takeovers was avoided by most companies, as they believed that acquisitions were costly, time-consuming, and complex enough without adding this extra dimension of difficulty.

Discussion

The decision to undertake a hostile takeover was made by the CEO with approval of the board of directors. Because of the inherent difficulties in completing a hostile takeover successfully, management spent a great deal of time to ensure that the acquisition would ultimately be successful.

The most common reasons given for undertaking a hostile takeover were:

1. There was no intention of retaining the candidate's management.

2. The acquirer was very familiar with the candidate's business and could replace management easily.

3. The acquirer considered the stock market value low enough to compensate for the risks involved.

Summary

The purpose of this study was to uncover the acquisition decision-making process followed by corporations in order to answer the question, "How does the acquisition decision-making process work in actual practice?" The emphasis in this study was on the decisions made in the process.

The normative model sets out an acquisition process made up of steps necessary to complete acquisitions. Although these steps were found to reflect the general acquisition process followed in practice accurately, readers might wrongly draw the conclusion that if all the steps are completed the process with be successful, ignoring the dynamic nature of the process. Companies that were successful acquirers completed the steps and put them into operation in a way that allowed decisions to be made on an effective and timely basis. The key to success is to make these decisions on a timely basis so as to maintain momentum during the acquisition process. The empirical models discussed in Chapter 4 include flowcharts that set out two examples of decision processes; these empirical models also are compared with the normative model.

Chapter 4

Empirical Models

In the empirical research we found that the acquisition decision-making process was similar for all companies examined. Each company, however, had an approach to acquisitions unique to its management style, organizational structure, and corporate culture. Therefore, to assist our readers in understanding what an acquisition decision-making process might look like, we present two flowchart examples of empirical models in this chapter.

One fundamental difference we found was the extent of the involvement of the CEO in the acquisition process. There were extremes of involvement, from a direct "hands on" approach, in which the CEO was a direct member of the acquisition team working closely with his senior executives (Example 2), to the more structured approach, in which much of the process was delegated to others in the organization (Example 1). We have tried to reflect these two extremes in our two examples. It should be emphasized that for the successful acquirers, even in the more formal and structured approach (Example 1), the involvement of the CEO and his senior executives was no less important to being successful. Thus those companies with the more structured approach still had a clear sense of purpose and direction communicated by the CEO, who made himself available for key decisions in the process.

The two examples reflect extremes in the ways companies we interviewed organized themselves to make acquisitions. Example 1 reflects the highly structured approach and Example 2 reflects the least structured approach.

Empirical Model—Example 1

Figure 6 is Example 1, presented as a flowchart of a highly structured approach used by the companies we interviewed to

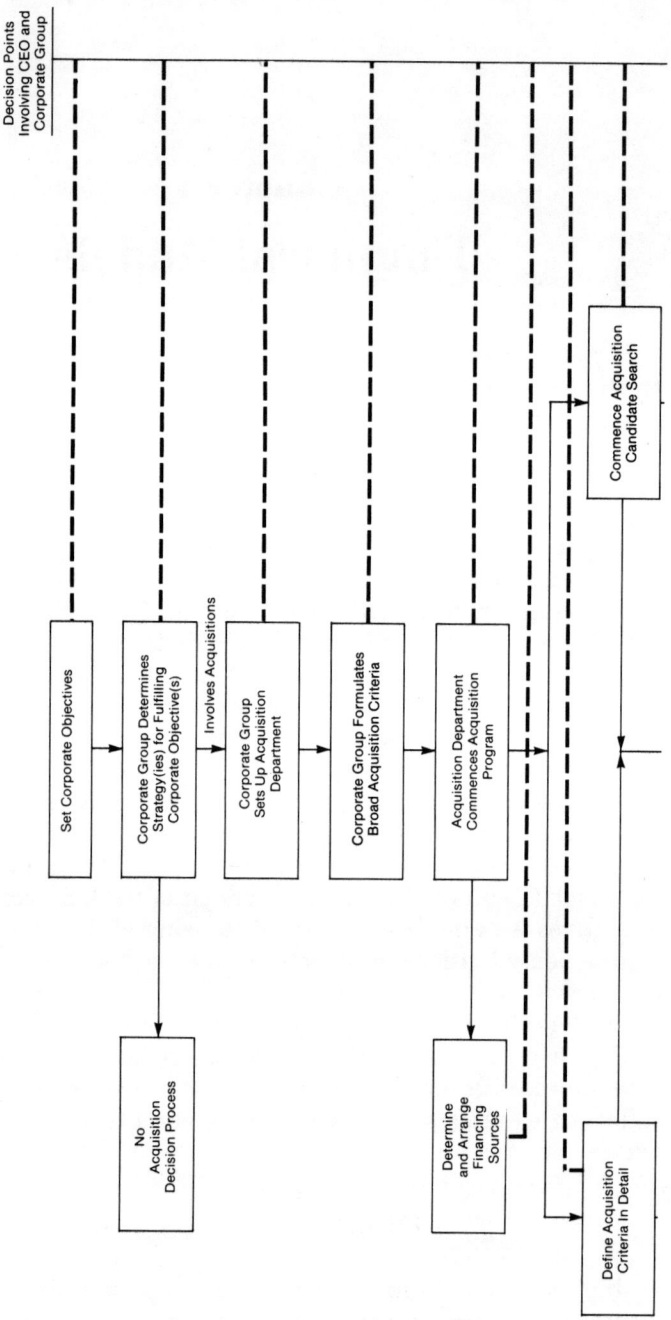

Figure 6
EMPIRICAL MODEL
EXAMPLE 1

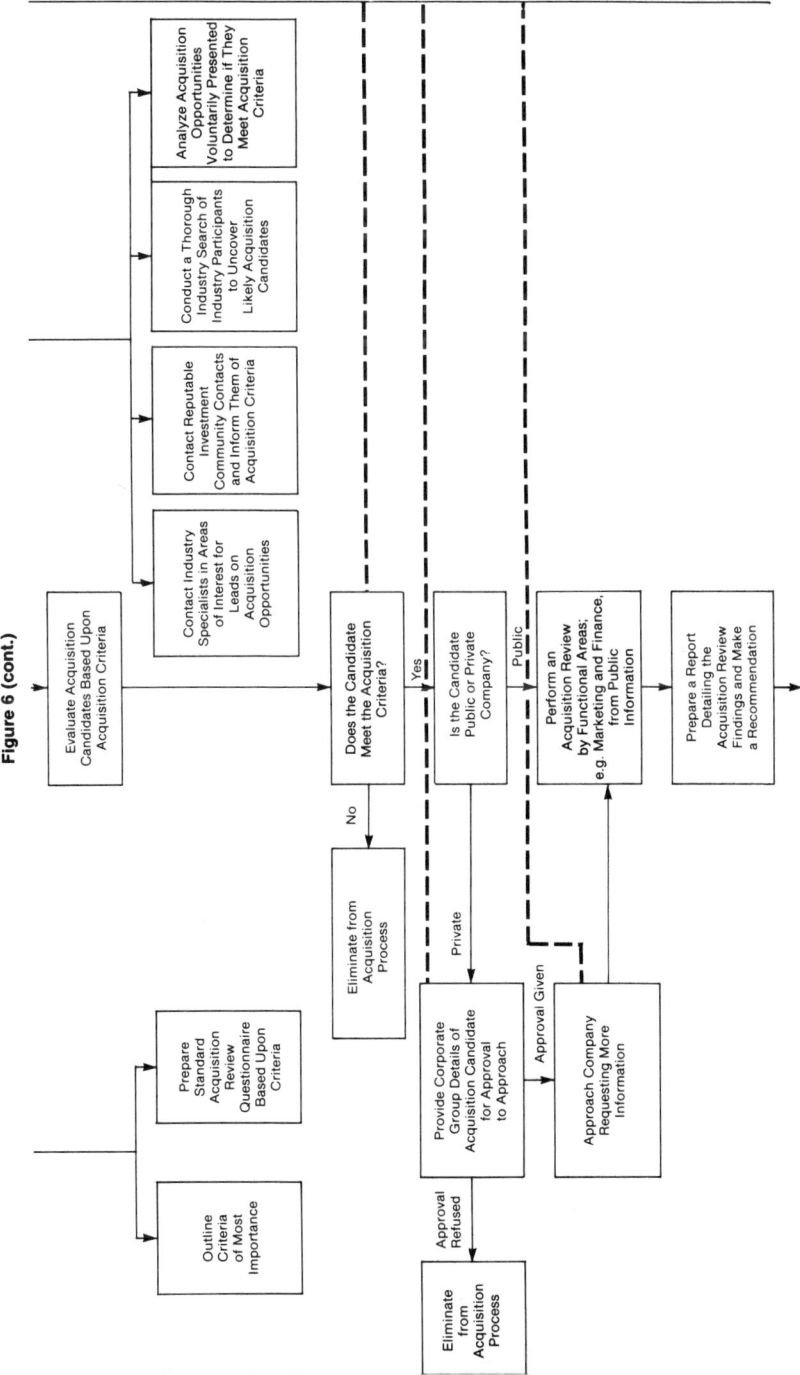

Figure 6 (cont.)

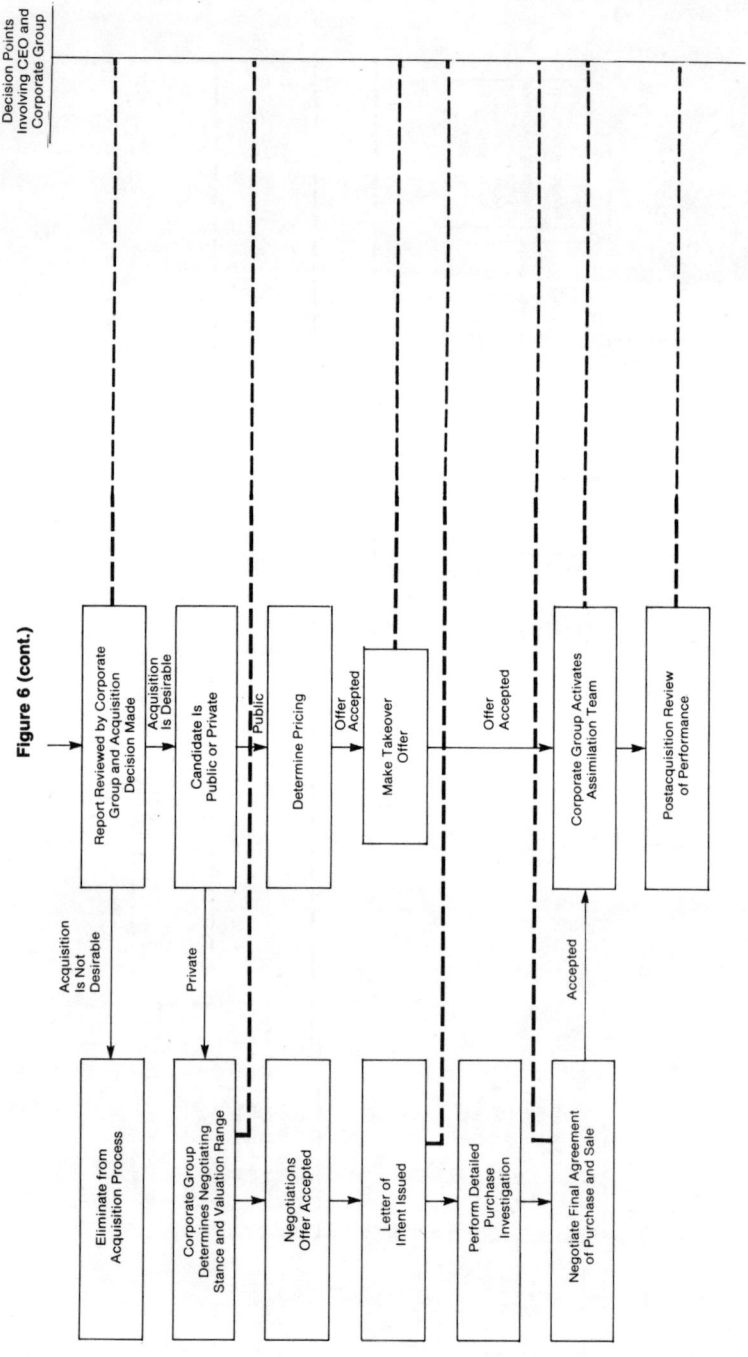

Figure 6 (cont.)

organize themselves for making acquisitions. Under this structure, the acquisition process begins when the corporate group—made up of the CEO and his senior vice presidents (including as a minimum the vice president of finance and vice president of corporate development)— decide what the company's corporate objectives will be. They would have these corporate objectives approved by the board of directors.

Once the objectives are approved by the board, the corporate group then determines what strategies it will use to achieve these objectives. If one of the strategies is for the company to undertake acquisitions, this strategy is usually presented to the board of directors for approval. If the strategic plan is approved, the corporate group commences to set up a full-time acquisition department (principally by hiring a vice president of corporate development) and establishes the broad acquisition criteria that will be used to segregate prospective candidates it wishes to pursue from candidates that are of no interest.

At the same time that the acquisition department begins an active search for acquisition candidates, the vice president of finance determines the optimum financing package and arranges for the financing to be available when needed. The package and the arrangements are approved by the corporate group.

In this model we have indicated the key decision points at which the CEO and his senior executives (the corporate group) would be involved, because it appeared to us that the great risk in adopting the highly structured approach is that the corporate group might abdicate rather than delegate its responsibilities for the acquisition process to the full-time acquisition specialists in the acquisition department. It was evident to us that the success of the acquisition process depended on the corporate group making certain it was actively involved in the key decisions throughout the process.

It is usual for the acquisition department to undertake an "active" search for suitable acquisition candidates. This would include not only keeping in close touch with industry specialists and members of the investment community, but also making a thorough and organized search of all companies carrying on business in the desired area of expansion interest. The department would also review all prospects voluntarily presented to the company by business brokers and other financial intermediaries.

Concurrent with starting a search for prospective candidates, the acquisition department would develop the more detailed acquisition criteria, usually of a financial nature, that would be applied in later stages of the evaluation of acquisition candidates.

Once a candidate had been identified that met the broad acquisition criteria, it was usual for the head of the acquisition department to review the prospect with the corporate group and request approval to approach the owner of the prospect. The corporate group was usually involved in deciding who in the company should make the initial approach. The flowcharts in both examples show the extremes in the level of analysis conducted. One extreme is represented by the private company acquisition, where detailed information is always sought and an in-depth review always undertaken. The second extreme is represented by an unsolicited offer for a public company, where any review must be made principally from publically available information.

In the case of a private company, the acquirer, on the initial approach to the owners of the prospect, tries to determine first that the company can be purchased and second that it can be purchased at an acceptable price. If these issues can be resolved favorably, a more detailed evaluation will be made on the basis of information furnished by the prospect.

A report on the basis of this analysis will be prepared, comparing the findings with both the broad and the detailed criteria that have been established. A recommendation will then be made to the corporate group on whether or not to pursue the opportunity. In the case of an unsolicited public offer the recommendation will be whether or not to make the offer. If an unsolicited offer is to be made, no further review will be conducted. The CEO and board of directors typically approve the offer price.

In the case of a private company, if the decision is made to pursue the candidate further, many acquirers will issue a nonbinding letter of intent for the prospect to agree to. If agreed to, the letter of intent provides for access to the company's accounts and records for the purpose of conducting a detailed purchase investigation.

The detailed purchase investigation will focus on determining whether the candidate continues to meet the acquisition criteria, whether the basis of valuation used in the letter of intent is still valid, and whether specific areas of concern need to be identified that will affect the price. A final report will be made to the corporate group before negotiation of a binding agreement of purchase and sale is begun.

If the offer is accepted, the corporate group will appoint a team of people to work with counterparts in the acquired company to implement an assimilation plan. Although many companies indicated that an assimilation plan should be started as early as possible in the acquisition process, it was apparent that the urgency of negotiations usually meant that such a plan was not developed until the deal was almost completed. As a result, developing the plan became part of the job of the assimilation team.

The final stage of the process was to conduct a review of how the acquisition had worked and to make a determination of what went right, what went wrong, and why. Conceptually the review is used to assess past acquisition practices of the company to improve future performance. The extent to which this is adequately done in most cases was uncertain from the interviews we conducted.

Empirical Model—Example 2

Figure 7, as Example 2, presents a flowchart of the least structured approach used by the companies we interviewed. In this example there is no full-time acquisition department. The acquisition team is made up from members of the corporate group. As can be seen from a comparison with Example 1, the same tasks and decisions are required in both approaches.

What characterizes this approach of a company toward organizing itself to make acquisitions is the active interest and involvement of the CEO in the entire acquisition process. This "hands on" approach and ability to make decisions quickly appeared to account in large measure for the success of companies using this approach in making acquisitions.

Comparison of Empirical Models with Normative Model

The normative acquisition decision model as described in Appendix A and included in *Normative Models in Managerial Decision-Making* summarizes the activities and decisions that make up the acquisition process as reflected in the literature on acquisitions. We found from the interviews conducted that the normative model accurately captures the tasks involved in the acquisition process. The normative model is comprehensive in this regard and we would say that companies generally adhere to this model in carrying out their acquisition programs.

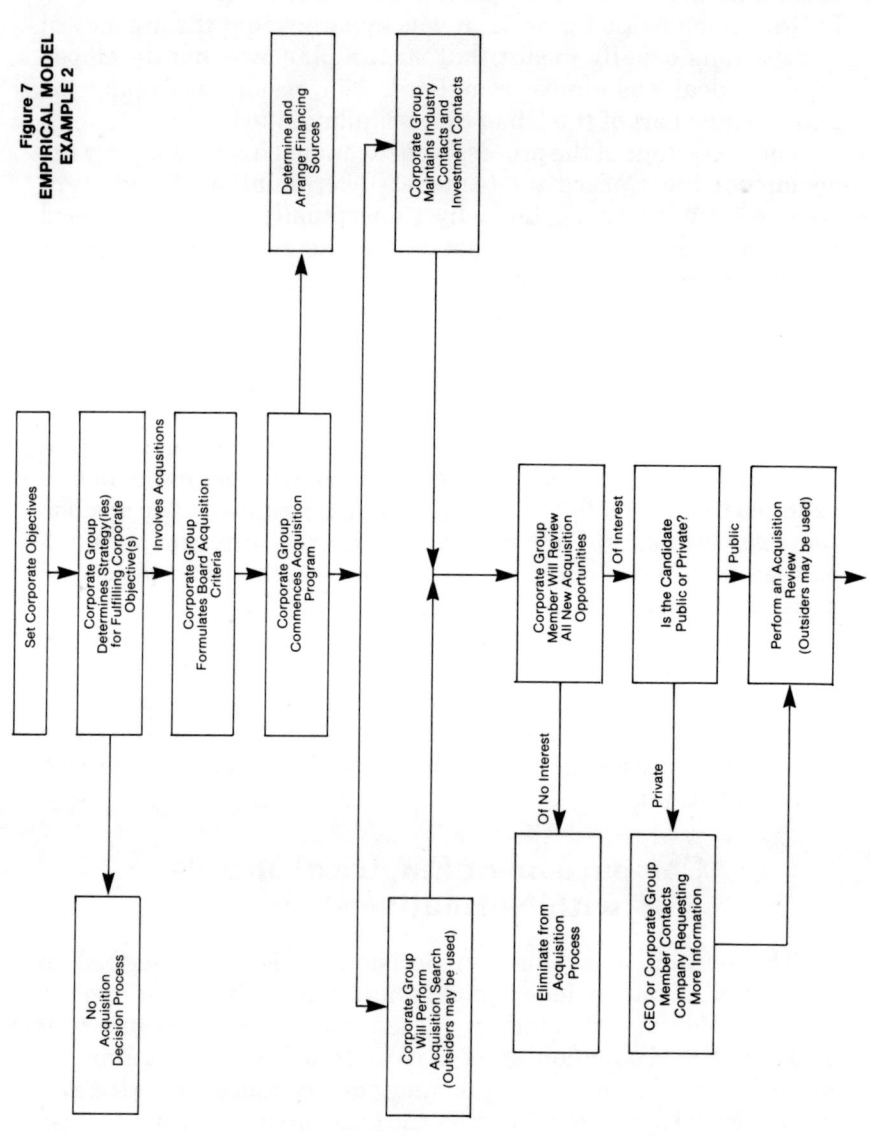

Figure 7
EMPIRICAL MODEL
EXAMPLE 2

Figure 7 (cont.)

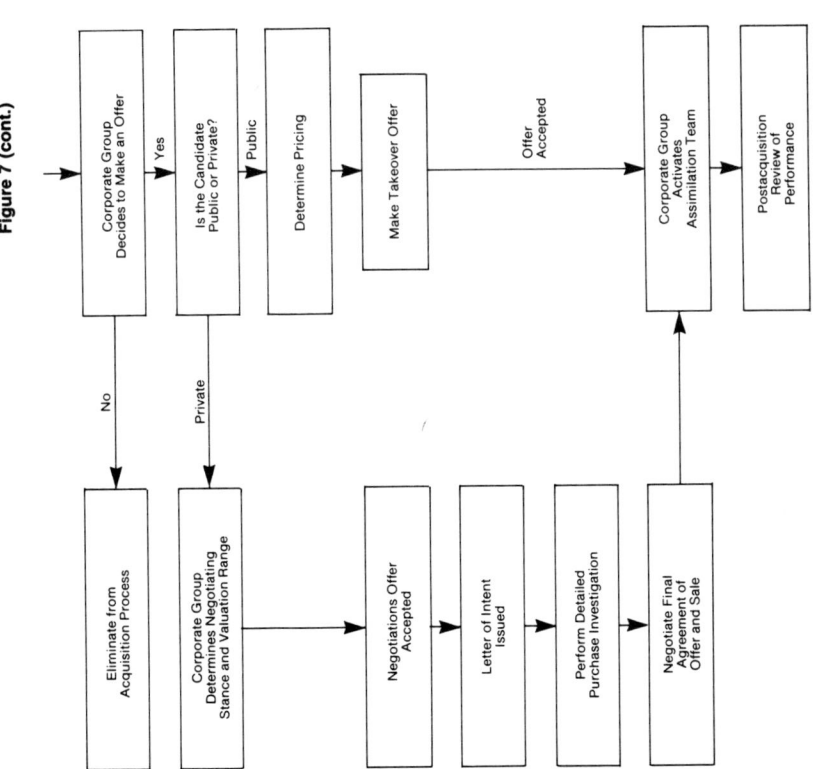

The normative model lists 27 individual tasks and decisions that make up the acquisition process. The various tasks and decisions in our empirical models compared with the normative model as follows.

Set Corporate Objectives

Both models start with the setting of objectives.

Determine Strategies

The normative model contained three steps that we include under the general task of determining strategies. The three steps in the normative model were:

• Determine if the objective could be realized better by acquisitions (Step 2).
• Assess alternatives that would be more useful than acquisitions in this respect (Step 3).
• Make policy decision on acquisitions (Step 4).

We felt that most companies undertake an extensive analysis of the optimum strategies that will be used to achieve overall corporate objectives. Many factors might lead to the decision to undertake acquisitions. Furthermore, acquisitions may become the principal strategy or just one of many strategies that will be used. If the result of the determination of appropriate strategies is that acquisitions are desirable, the next step is to activate an acquisition program.

Set up Acquisition Department

The next step in the acquisition process corresponds with Step 9 in the normative model—"Assign responsibility for acquisitions analysis and decisions." The model of the less structured approach had a full-time acquisition department, and this responsibility was assigned on an ad hoc basis to deal with an evaluation of specific acquisition candidates.

We included this step before determining acquisition criteria because the vice president of corporate development hired to head the acquisition department is frequently asked to assist in the development of acquisition criteria.

Formulate Broad Acquisition Criteria

The process of developing acquisition criteria is covered in Steps 5 to 8 of the normative model, which included:

- Consider objectives (Step 5).
- Examine firm's strategies (Step 6).
- Assess firm's weaknesses (Step 7).
- Arrive at criteria to be met by acquisitions (Step 8).

In our model we showed the setting of broad criteria and detailed criteria. The narrative to the normative model also indicated that both levels of criteria setting would be involved.

Determine and Arrange Financing Sources

Step 11 in the normative model is "Assess if the firm is now in a position to acquire (sufficient resources)." Much later in the process, and almost concurrent with the decision to acquire a particular company, Step 24 of the normative model is "Decide on financing arrangements." In our empirical model we chose to emphasize determining the availability of financing and arranging for financing very early in the process, as we found that most companies, once they had decided to make acquisitions, immediately looked for funds and arranged for them to be available.

Timing

The normative model indicated as a separate step, Step 13, "Decide on timing of acquisitions." Step 12 was another item related to timing—"See if the firm requires new competences or market outlets immediately." The notes elaborating on the normative model flowchart indicated that the urgency to make a deal could affect the process. We found that the acquisition process was so dynamic that the question of timing was pertinent almost throughout the process, was assessed at every stage, and was affected by many factors. We did not feel it could be reflected in a flowchart form.

Search for Candidate

This is dealt with in the normative model in Step 10, "Determine if alternative acquisition possibilities now available," and Step 15, "Locate and screen acquisition possibilities until firm (or firms) is found which meets defined criteria."

Evaluation and Negotiation

Steps 16 through 23 in the normative model deal with the areas of evaluation and negotiation. These items did not reflect what we found to be three levels of evaluation and negotiation, going from initial selection and contact, to a more detailed review and issue of a letter of intent, to an in-depth purchase investigation and completion of an agreement of purchase and sale. We feel that the empirical model reflects the interrelationship of the evaluation made and the negotiations that took place in the course of completing a deal.

Assimilation

In the empirical model the assimilation team would cover Step 26 in the normative model—"Postacquisition appraisal of new firm—From the Inside," and Step 27, "Design Integration Plan."

Postacquisition Review

The empirical model includes as part of the acquisition process a much later review of whether or not the acquisition worked out for the purchaser. As stated in the report, although most believed that such an after-the-fact assessment should be part of the process, it was uncertain to what extent the review was effectively built into most acquisition programs.

General Deficiency of Models

Because of the dynamic nature of the acquisition process and its general complexity, we feel that flowchart models of the process do not tell much about the true nature of the process and by their very nature make the process look somewhat mechanical. As we hope this report shows, there is nothing mechanical about the process as carried out by successful acquirers.

Appendix A

Normative Model*

The literature on acquisition (merger) decisions is quite extensive and, for the most part, global in scope. For example, in many instances there are discussions of the fundamental goals of the acquiring organization, analyses of its strengths and weaknesses, and so forth. Probably the far-reaching consequences of the acquisition decision are responsible for so broad an orientation.

No major discrepancies or "schools" could be found in the normative acquisition literature. Only variations in the emphasis of certain steps were noted. More specifically, some articles stressed the importance of a postacquisition plan for integrating the new firm into the conglomerate, while others cursorily passed over this step. Some viewed assignment of responsibilities for the acquisition decision as an explicit part of the decision, while others seemed to assume that this had already occurred once and for all.

Figure 8 and the accompanying explication derive from the general nature of the information contained in the normative literature rather than from any specific source.

Elaboration on the Flowchart

1. Consider and define the objectives of the firm. This step is essential as acquisitions should help the firm attain these objectives. The clarification of objectives can stem from discussions among top management and owners of the firm and should guide the acquisition decision.

2-3. Establish the utility of the acquisition as a basic tool in helping to achieve objectives. For example, if it is the goal

*Excerpt chapter from *Normative Models in Managerial Decision-Making,* Lawrence A. Gordon, Danny Miller, and Henry Mintzberg, 1975.

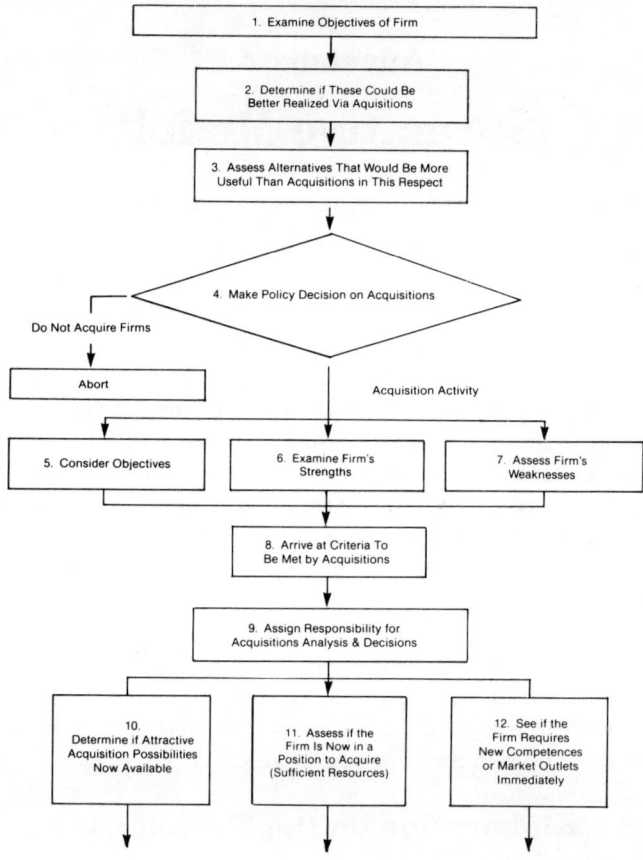

Figure 8
NORMATIVE MODEL

Figure 8 (cont.)

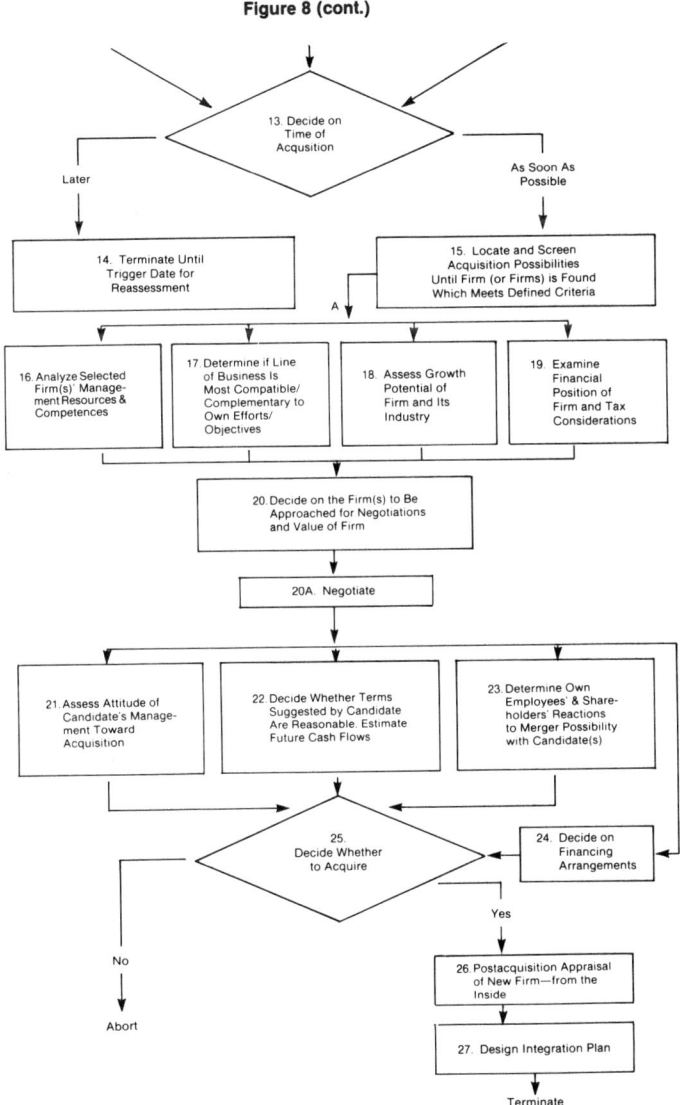

of a firm to grow in a certain area, acquisitions might be a useful tactic. If, however, immediate profitability is a superordinate goal, strategies other than acquisitions might be most appropriate. The firm's own past experiences with acquisitions, the results of acquisition strategies of competitors, and the advice of financial or acquisition specialists will provide clues on the overall merits of making an acquisition.

4.   Make a policy decision on acquisitions. In the light of the firm's goals and its cursory research into the general advantages and limitations of acquisitions in terms of its financial situation, decide whether to continue to entertain acquisition as a potential tactic.

5.   Set up broad objectives that pertain directly to the acquisition decision. That is, establish a list of the basic desired characteristics of acquisition candidates. Such a list may be constructed on the basis of the firm's marketing, financial, and production resources and aspirations. Input about these aspirations may come from executive opinions, policy manuals, functional department heads, and the like.

6.   Examine the firm's strengths. Acquisitions should complement the firm's strengths. These might be assessed by establishing the products that are successful, the financial reserves of the firm, the unique skills available to the company that give it a particular competitive advantage, profitable market segments that might be exploited better via some acquisition, and other pertinent factors. The search and analysis necessary for carrying out this step can focus on financial statements, sales reports, marketing department appraisals of sales territories or target markets, and so forth.

7.   Examine the firm's weaknesses and limitations, using basically the same type of approach as that advocated in Step 6.

8.   Establish more *specific* criteria acquisition candidates must meet in the light of the objectives, strengths, and weaknesses identified in Steps 5, 6, and 7, respectively. For example, the firm might discover that a major weak-

ness is in the form of inadequate sources of supply, while a key strength is the technical expertise presently on hand to set up efficient production processes. An objective of the firm might then be to procure a company that produces the raw materials or parts required for its production process. Furthermore, if the firm has a product that is subject to cyclical market demand fluctuations, it may look for an acquisition candidate whose product's sales "dovetail" with its own. A list of such criteria should emerge from the list of objectives, strengths, and weaknesses evolved.

9. Top management should assign responsibility for analyzing and screening acquisition possibilities. It would be sensible to include people from a multitude of disciplines in a body that would deal with proposed acquisitions. If, for example, the prime purpose of an acquisition is, according to established objectives, to obtain a more useful marketing facility, the body should have strong marketing representation. Care must be taken to ensure that authority patterns as portrayed on the organization chart are not violated to any great extent in the acquisition analysis body's reporting pattern.

10. Determine if attractive acquisition candidates exist in light of established criteria. This task should be performed by the acquisition group in consultation with investment dealers, financial report surveys, informal meetings with competitors, and so on.

11. Determine if the firm has enough resources to acquire the desirable acquisition candidate. A financial analysis must be undertaken to establish the repercussions of the acquisition on the present and projected asset, debt, and equity positions.

12. It is important to determine how urgently the firm must acquire the candidate. For example, one may consider to what extent the firm requires a new product, market, management group, technical resource, or whatever immediately and whether it can afford to wait a while. Marketing, personnel, costing, and interim financial reports can be used in deciding the urgency of the situa-

tion. Another key factor that may influence the advantages of immediate acquisition is the general availability of alternative candidates.

13.   On the basis of Steps 10 to 12, decide on the timing of the acquisition.

14.   If it is decided to defer the matter, postpone investigation to a specific future date and recycle to Step 10.

15.   If it is decided to proceed as soon as possible with the acquisition, locate and screen several candidates. Using the sources cited in Step 10, find acquisition candidate(s) and make a rough cut at deciding if prospect(s) might be worthwhile to follow up by comparing its (their) basic features with criteria established in Step 8.

16.   Analyze in detail selected candidate(s), focusing on its (their) management resources and skills. Establish whether managers seem in tune with current trends in the industry. Find out if they have been competent in adapting their organization to its environment. Consider any special skills or technical knowledge that the candidate might have that could prove useful to the parent company. Information on these factors could be gathered by interviews with the management of the candidate and records of its past performance.

17.   Determine compatibility of candidate's orientations. One can proceed, for example, by examining the determinants of market demand for the candidate's products (look for synergy in distribution channels and promotional efforts) or by regarding the benefits of increased economies of scale that might stem from a merger of production facilities. Marketing and production specialists in both the candidate's and one's own firm can provide insights on compatibilities.

18.   Assess candidate's growth potential by examining the sales, profit, and market growth rates of the firm and its industry. Financial and market forecasts prepared by impartial parties might be the best source of information.

19.   Examine the financial position of the candidate by inspecting such things as current and debt-to-equity

ratios, past and projected earnings, and the state of capital equipment. Financial statements and records and plant tours also would be useful in this respect.

20. Decide on firms to be approached and arrive at a preliminary estimate of a fair price to pay. The decision could be made by weighting the information considered in Steps 16 to 19 in order of importance. Weighting can be done by a group of people whose assigned scores are averaged in some manner. Each weighted dimension must receive a rating. Aggregate ratings can be prepared for each candidate being considered. Those candidates who do best should once again be assessed by experts on the acquisition team in order to establish a reasonable bid price.

21. Assess attitude of candidate's management toward acquisition. Determine if executives seem motivated to become part of a larger corporate endeavor by interviewing these people. If not, decide whether their reluctance will pose serious problems to a successful integration of the firms.

22. Find out if candidate is willing to accept bid price. Discover if candidate is willing to consider a price close to that offered. If not, find out why. Decide if some rapprochement can be achieved.

23. Examine the climate within own firm to specific acquisition proposal. What do shareholders and employees think? Do their feelings represent an obstacle to a successful integration of the firms?

24. Decide on financing arrangements. Expert counsel should be obtained in determining the cheapest or most efficient method of financing the acquisition. Consider costs of debt and equity financing, legal restrictions, risks of alternative methods, long-term effects on earnings, and so on.

25. Using the techniques and approach discussed in Step 20, decide whether or not to make the acquisition.

26. Do a postacquisition appraisal. Go through Steps 16, 17, 18, 19, and 21 again, this time obtaining an insider's view of the state of the new acquisition. This is essential for

establishing the constraints and opportunities that must be considered in order to devise a plan for integrating the firms.

27.   Design integration plan. Use information gathered in Step 26 to design an approach for integrating, where desirable, the operations of the acquired and parent firms. Some key questions that must be answered are:

- Should you replace new firm's top management?
- Should you close down inefficient facilities (theirs or yours)?
- Should you combine similar production processes under one roof?
- Should you reorient distribution channels?

Expert personnel in functional areas must help perform such an analysis.

Appendix B

Summary of Responses to Questionnaire

In this appendix we discuss the nature of the responses received during the interviews and the reason for posing individual questions. The questions were set out in the consolidated questionnaire under major topic areas.

The topic areas included in the questionnaire were:

- Corporate Objectives
- Corporate Strategies
- Acquisition Criteria
- Acquisition Team
- Acquisition Search Methods
- Acquisitions in Foreign Jurisdictions
- Evaluation of Acquisition Candidates
- Negotiations and the Final Decision
- Financing the Acquisition
- Review of the Company's Acquisition Activities
- Reflections, Past and Present

Corporate Objectives

A. *Does the company have formalized corporate objectives?*

With this question we were trying to find out whether successful acquirers had well-articulated corporate objectives. The use of the word "formalized" was intended to find out whether the company's objectives had been written down and whether the company had taken formal action to approve or adopt the objectives.

There did not appear to be any consistency in formalizing objectives. Some companies had their corporate objectives approved by the board of directors. Others had no formal procedure for approving overall corporate objectives. In the United States most public companies did have publicly stated corporate objectives. In large measure, this practice appeared to result from requirements of the contents of Form 10K filed with the Securities and Exchange Commission and the fact that as a general practice public companies include statements on corporate objectives in annual reports.

All companies interviewed had clearly understood corporate objectives regardless of whether or not such objectives were "formalized." (Had the question been "Does the company have well-defined corporate objectives?" the answer would have been "yes" for all companies interviewed.)

B. *Who is primarily responsible for developing these corporate objectives?*

In almost all cases we found that the CEO was principally responsible for developing corporate objectives. In many cases he was solely responsible for developing these objectives. In a few cases a new CEO had been hired by the board of directors, and his overriding initial mandate was to define or redefine the firm's corporate objectives. Frequently the redefinition of corporate objectives resulted in the firm becoming an active acquirer for the first time.

There seems to be wide variation in the extent of the involvement of others in addition to the CEO in the process of developing and agreeing on corporate objectives. In many cases the board of directors was heavily involved in the process. This involvement appeared to be greatest in private companies or in public companies that had significant individual shareholdings. In these cases the relationship of the CEO and the board tended to be of an open participatory nature. This degree of participation by the board of directors did not appear to affect the CEO's view that he was primarily responsible for developing and setting corporate objectives.

We also found that there was no consistency in the extent to which the CEO involved other senior executives in this decision-making process. To a large degree we believe that this involvement was directly a function of the CEO's management style. Those whose style appeared to be authoritarian tended to listen to their own voice, whereas those who had a more open and participatory management style appeared to seek a heavy involvement of their senior management team in the process. In some cases the CEO hired outsiders to assist in developing an overall strategic plan for the company.

Some highly diversified companies and conglomerates that carried on a number of different businesses and that had separate presidents of the major divisions or subsidiaries moved the process described above one level down, with the CEO of the overall company acting more in the role of the board of directors.

C. *Who approves these objectives?*

The standard answer to this question was that the board of directors had ultimate responsibility for approving corporate objectives. This question did not elicit a great deal of response; we sensed, as noted previously, that the critical issue was not whether the objectives had been formalized in the sense of being documented.The suggestion that comes from the concept of "approval" as used in this question is that the process of setting corporate objectives is in some way formalized by an approval process.

Again, the critical issue is that such objectives exist and are well defined. The other critical aspect of the acquisition process that came through in the interviews was that, in addition to well-defined corporate objectives existing, they be known and understood. A most critical function of the CEO was his role in ensuring that not only the employees, but he too, clearly understood the firm's corporate objectives. In terms of the acquisition process it appeared essential for everyone involved in the process to have this knowledge and understanding, whether they were senior executives or outside consultants. This communication and this understanding meant much to the success of the undertaking.

D. *What is the process by which these objectives are updated and revised?*

The typical answer was that the company's corporate objectives are updated on an ongoing basis. Most of the respondents did not have a fast answer and responded, either directly or indirectly, with the sense of "Well, I guess this just happens on an ongoing basis."

Our view is that most successful acquirers have at one time spent a great deal of time and effort in establishing their objectives, and having done so have stuck to them. This consistency of objectives seems to be a distinguishing mark of successful acquirers. They do not tend to be companies that are constantly reviewing what or who they should be.

It appears that once these firms have set their corporate objectives and defined them clearly, they are unlikely to make frequent changes. In many cases, a major reassessment of corporate objectives was a preliminary step leading to the decision to acquire.

E. *Are these objectives known to the public?*

We wanted to find out whether successful acquirers generally tried to make their objectives known to the public and whether they might in some way have this characteristic in common. There was a wide variation in corporate policy and preference on this point. Some companies consciously tried to have their corporate objectives kept confidential. These companies appeared to feel that their objectives were an integral part of their strategic plan and that for competitive reasons it was important that the public not know what their plans were.

Others took great care to make sure that their corporate objectives were widely publicized and well known. Some companies did this purposely because they felt that the public awareness made more acquisition opportunities available to them. They felt that the widespread knowledge of their corporate objectives and the fact that they were active acquirers resulted in opportunities being voluntarily presented to them of which they might not otherwise have become aware.

Corporate Strategies

A. *Who is primarily responsible for developing the strategies that will be used to achieve corporate objectives?*

It appears that the development and setting of corporate strategies parallel very closely the setting of corporate objectives, except that the process is generally moved one step down in the corporate structure.

The development of corporate strategies tends not to involve the board of directors substantially; it is done more by the CEO in conjunction with other senior officers. Frequently these strategies are developed by a corporate head office group working together. In highly diversified or conglomerate companies specific strategies to achieve objectives are frequently developed at the divisional or subsidiary level representing each business unit.

The involvement of the CEO in the strategy formulation process varied considerably, but all successful acquirers had sufficient CEO involvement to ensure that the strategies were the most appropriate for achieving the company's objectives. It appeared that where acquisitions became a principal corporate strategy, the CEO's involvement was mandatory. In many cases the involvement of the CEO in the process of developing corporate strategies allowed the senior officers to become intimately familiar with the CEO's views of the company's corporate objectives. This communication link between those to be involved in the acquisition process that was developed in the course of establishing agreed-upon corporate strategies was, as indicated in the discussion of corporate objectives, a critical part of the acquisition process.

Where the company had a full-time acquisition department, the vice president of corporate development and his staff were frequently responsible for the initial development of the corporate strategies to be adopted.

B. *Who approves these strategies?*

The CEO was principally involved in approving corporate strategies. Most companies indicated, however, that the board of directors could be part of the approval process, particularly where acquisitions were part of that overall strategy.

Strategies of less significance to the total corporate organization might be approved at the subsidiary or divisional level, with only major strategic choices requiring approval by the corporate-level CEO. The decision to seek acquisitions would be considered a major strategic choice.

C. *How are these strategies updated and revised?*

The typical answer was that corporate strategies were "updated and revised on an ongoing basis." In most cases they really seemed to be done on an ongoing informal basis and were a natural outflow of the planning process.

Although corporate strategies in most companies were not updated and revised on the basis of a preconceived formalized approach, our understanding is that when the corporate objectives are changed or revised, they are likely to require a corresponding adjustment to corporate strategies. Further, corporate strategies could change without a corresponding change in objectives, but this change would require prior introspective examination to assess a new optimal approach to satisfying corporate objectives.

D. *Are these strategies generally known in the financial community?*

As in the comparable question under corporate objectives, we were trying to assess whether public knowledge of corporate strategies had any bearing on being a successful acquirer. In contrast to the response for corporate objectives, it was found that most companies did not make their specific corporate strategies known to the financial community.

However, when making acquisitions was one of the corporate strategies, this fact was generally made known to the financial community as part of the company's plan to attract and be made aware of acquisition opportunities. Informing financial community members was usually done through individual contacts of the CEO and others. Such contacts included investment banking and brokerage firms. Companies would also inform publishers of acquisition and divestiture newsletters and the financial press in general.

Some companies relied almost entirely upon this network of contacts for acquisition prospects, while others relied more on their own internal search. The two methods were not mutually exclusive. Even those companies performing extensive organized searches benefited from their wide range of informal contacts and made certain that such contacts were aware of their corporate acquisition strategy and acquisition criteria. Our observation was that acquirers with a track record of making acquisitions were generally known in the financial community and elsewhere to be active acquirers, and this fact was of great benefit in terms of the number of opportunities presented to them.

E. *Have acquisitions been a primary strategy to achieve the company's corporate objectives?*

Since all the companies interviewed were active acquirers, it is understandable that the response was unanimous that acquisitions had been a primary strategy for achieving their corporate objectives. Although the response appears obvious, we asked this question for two reasons: first, to confirm that our assessment of the particular company as an active acquirer was correct, and second, to see if that company perceived itself as such. Some indicated that acquisitions were just one strategy and that growth by internal investment was of equal importance.

F. *What is your company's objective for seeking acquisitions? (Examples: growth, diversification, stability, rejuvenation, and/or profitability.)*

The three main reasons given by companies for seeking acquisitions were:

1. Increased profitability
2. Growth
3. Diversification

Since shareholders expect profits to increase from year to year and use this as an indicator of management's performance, most companies were of the opinion that they have to continue improving their profitability. By maintaining growth, most companies felt that they were hedging against the possibility that a lack of growth might in fact lead to a decline in overall size and profitability.

Diversification by acquisition was typically selected because it was easier to acquire in-place management, assets, and technological expertise than it was to establish a new business. This was particularly true for businesses in which the company did not have prior experience.

G. *Can you elaborate on your answer to question F above, to highlight the reasons your company has chosen acquisitions as a corporate strategy?*

A common reason for acquisitions was that companies had an excess of cash available to them and expansion through acquisition was a logical way to invest the cash flow.

The reasons provided for undertaking acquisitions differed among companies, but the most frequent responses were:

1. The ability to acquire an ongoing company for less than the cost of starting a similar operation.
2. The ability to use an inexpensive and sure method of gaining market share.
3. The ability to acquire management expertise and/or new technology, with little time expended by their own management team.

The above-noted reasons may in some cases reflect the current state of the economy and stock market at any particular time. The rationale might change in differing economic climates. In all cases the overriding rationale for undertaking acquisitions was to fulfill corporate objectives.

H.   *Who determines in what circumstances acquisitions are likely to be the most effective strategy to achieve particular objectives?*

This question was intended to provide a greater understanding of how the decision was made that acquisitions were the best strategy. The responses were similar to the responses to question A in this section, "Who is primarily responsible for developing the strategies that will be used to achieve corporate objectives?" Respondents did not provide further insight into the decision-making process, but commented once again on the involvement of the CEO in strategy formulation. This may be significant, as we observed that the desire and determination of the CEO to make acquisitions were consistent in the successful acquirers we interviewed.

This question served as an introduction to the next topic area, and respondents went on to explain that once acquisitions had been decided upon as a basic strategy for meeting corporate objectives, the senior officers involved in strategy formulation would establish the broad acquisition criteria to ensure that any acquisition to be considered would satisfy corporate objectives. Where a vice president of corporate development was to be hired, he might assist in developing these criteria. It was emphasized that the CEO was primarily responsible for approving such criteria.

Acquisition Criteria

A.   *Has the company developed acquisition criteria which it applies in assessing acquisition candidates?*

All the companies we interviewed had a broad definition of acquisition criteria to guide them in their initial assessment of acquisition candidates. The nature of these criteria varied widely and depended upon the type of acquisition and the reasons for making the acquisition. As with corporate objectives, there seemed to be no consistency between companies as to whether these criteria were "formalized" or not. Companies that had full-time acquisition departments tended to have written criteria that could be used by members of that department in assessing candidates.

Most companies tended to use both broadly and narrowly defined acquisition criteria to assess acquisition candidates. This may have been significant in that the broad criteria, though precise enough to allow a quick identification of opportunities to be pursued (and, possibly of more importance, those not to be pursued) were not so narrow as to eliminate most opportunities. In other words, the broad criteria seemed to be realistic in the sense that they recognized that in the real world the "perfect acquisition" probably does not exist. The more narrowly defined detailed criteria were then used to eliminate some candidates initially identified as possible acquisition candidates.

Although not all companies set down their acquisition criteria formally in writing, it was clear that the companies interviewed had been successful in communicating these criteria to all those directly involved in making acquisitions.

B. *Who approves the acquisition criteria?*

The broad acquisition criteria discussed above generally were set and approved by the same group of senior corporate officers who were directly involved in setting corporate strategies. This corporate group would include the CEO and the vice presidents of finance, marketing, and corporate development.

The CEO was always an active member of the corporate group setting broad criteria and was directly involved in approving the criteria.

These broad acquisition criteria are then further refined. The more detailed criteria are often developed by the acquisition department, where there is one. The vice president of corporate development then has them approved by the corporate group. Examples of both broad criteria and detailed criteria are set out in Chapter 3 of the report.

C. *What is the process by which acquisition criteria are updated and revised?*

The broad acquisition criteria did not change significantly once they were developed. The revision of broad acquisition criteria usually reflected a change in corporate objectives or strategies.

Changes in the detailed criteria were not significant except to reflect current market conditions, such as swings in interest rates and required rates of return. These changes were implemented and approved by the head of the acquisition team.

D. *Who conducts the analysis to determine whether potential acquisition candidates meet the acquisition criteria?*

As was indicated previously, there are usually various levels of analysis to determine whether acquisition candidates meet the acquisition criteria. The first level of analysis is to determine if the candidate would be considered a potential acquisition (broad criteria); subsequent levels of analysis (detailed criteria) are made to determine whether to sign a letter of intent and ultimately to decide whether to sign a final offer of purchase and sale. Use of the detailed criteria generally involves the application of more rigorous financial and other tests.

Who performed the tests depended largely on whether the company had a full-time acquisition department. Where the company had such a department, it was usually headed by a vice president of corporate development. This vice president would be a member of the corporate group of senior officers who had overall responsibility for the acquisition program.

Members of this department included people with backgrounds and skills in a number of disciplines; for example, finance and marketing. There would also be people with knowledge and experience in valuing businesses. When such a department existed, most of the analysis—both in applying the broad criteria to make an initial identification of candidates and in performing the detailed analysis—was done by this department.

Where there was no full-time acquisition department, the corporate group generally made up the acquisition team and was constituted to do detailed reviews for particular acquisitions on an ad hoc basis. It was usual for each member of the team to take responsibility for particular aspects of the analysis that related to his area. One member of the group would be designated to pull all the analyses together. Frequently this overall responsibility would fall on the vice president of finance, although in some cases it could change, depending on the work loads of the members of the group.

Under each approach to structuring an acquisition review team, the review findings are compared with both the broad and the detailed criteria. In determining whether potential acquisition candidates initially meet the acquisition criteria, most of the companies interviewed emphasized the necessity of using broad acquisition criteria to eliminate candidates definitely not of interest to the company. This initial hurdle is set at a moderate height so that those judged not to have cleared it are unequivocally of no interest.

When it comes to applying detailed criteria, the involvement of the corporate group is minimized where there is a full-time acquisition department.

E. *Who determines that the result of the analysis warrants further investigation?*

Where the corporate group is the acquisition team, it is usual for this group to decide whether the candidate warrants a more detailed review.

Where a full-time acquisition department exists, the head of that department (usually the vice president of corporate development) decides if a particular candidate meets the broad acquisition criteria and therefore warrants further review. In most instances it would be usual for him to review this decision with the corporate group before proceeding to the more detailed review.

On completion of the detailed review the head of the acquisition department would present his department's analysis to the corporate group, usually in the form of a detailed report. He would recommend initially whether to issue a nonbinding letter of intent and finally whether to sign a legal agreement of purchase and sale and what the suggested terms of the agreement should be.

F. *At the point that a determination is made that a prospect meets your acquisition criteria, what approach is made to determine:*

(i) *Whether the company is available for sale?*

(ii) *Whether the company would consider you as the purchaser?*

The responses to these two questions tended to be interrelated and varied, depending somewhat upon the way in which the potential candidate came to the company's attention. Where the opportunity was brought to the company (for example, by a business broker or an investment banker), the fact that the business or company was for sale was obvious. However, when the opportunity had been identified by the company from its own internal search for candidates or when the candidate was suggested by an investment broker who did not represent it, it was our observation that most would first want to make a quick determination that the candidate met their broad acquisition criteria. Assuming that this hurdle was passed, most companies would then want to make a determination that the candidate was in fact for sale and would want to approach the principal decision maker as quickly as possible before spending time in making a detailed review.

The approach to the owners to determine if the company was for sale also enabled the acquirer to determine whether or not he would be viewed as an acceptable purchaser. The answer to the latter question was resolved by whether or not the prospect would provide the information necessary for the acquirer to make a more detailed assessment and formulate some kind of tentative offer.

An issue not dealt with in the questionnaire but that came up in some of the interviews was who made the initial approach to the prospective candidate. This appeared to vary, but, as a general rule, when the acquisition was significant or when the management of the company to be acquired would be a significant factor in deciding whether a deal would be made, the CEO frequently made the contact. Certainly any contact was generally made with the approval of the CEO. In some cases the CEO preferred not to be involved in the initial contacts and wished to be held in reserve until a more accurate determination could be made of whether there was a likelihood of making a deal.

G. *Would your company consider a hostile takeover?*

Because of the popularity of hostile takeovers in the early 1980s we thought it appropriate to examine this issue and its place in making an acquisition decision. Most companies stated that they would not consider a hostile takeover, and the few companies that indicated that they would consider making a hostile takeover qualified their answer.

Where the acquisition of a private company was contemplated, a hostile takeover was considered unlikely. In this type of situation, a deal would have to be made with shareholders of the private company. It was pointed out that management might be hostile to the takeover even when the shareholders were willing to sell.

Various reasons were given to justify undertaking a hostile takeover. These include:

1. Where there was no intention of retaining the candidate's management.

2. Where the acquirer was very familiar with the candidate's business and could easily replace existing management with its own.

3. Where the acquirer thought that the candidate was significantly undervalued and this fact more than compensated for the risks involved in a hostile takeover.

Most companies found acquisitions a difficult, expensive, and time-consuming process without adding the further complexity of it being hostile. Some companies saw a trend toward greater competition for candidates and felt hostile takeovers only resulted in an overinflated price for the candidate by attracting competitive bidders. Some companies stated that they had a policy against entering into any kind of bidding war for acquisitions.

Within the acquisition process the decision to make a hostile takeover is determined after the review of public information (since we are principally referring to a takeover of public companies) is complete. The decision itself is that of the corporate group and the board of directors because of the sensitivity of this issue.

H. *Under what circumstances does the company find it beneficial to make an unsolicited offer?*

This question can only apply in the case of publicly traded companies. Since an unsolicited offer is the method of carrying out a hostile takeover, the answers to question G above apply. However, it is possible to make a friendly unsolicited offer when the offer is made by an acquirer friendly to management that has not revealed its acquisition plans. Some companies mentioned that they tended to avoid such offers. Most companies liked to know in advance that their offer would be received favorably.

I. *Do the financial criteria relate to:*
  (i) rate of return?
  (ii) price/earnings multiple?
  (iii) other ratios?

This question was also intended to determine the extent to which financial criteria serve as a hurdle in the initial review of acquisition candidates as compared with other acquisition criteria and how such financial criteria are applied during the in-depth evaluation process.

Because of time constraints and the senior level of officers we were interviewing, the responses typically were quite general. We did not learn of any specific rules followed in particular situations, nor did we accumulate an exhaustive list of financial criteria actually applied in practice.

As stated previously, particularly in the case of private company acquisitions, detailed financial criteria generally were not included in the broad criteria used to determine initially if a company might be a logical candidate to acquire. Financial criteria were, however, a significant part of the more detailed acquisition criteria used to eliminate candidates that, from a financial perspective, were not likely to meet the return on investment demanded by the acquirer. The numerical criteria differed, depending on the industry sector being reviewed, since each requires a somewhat different rate of return and price/earnings multiple, according to current market conditions.

Although financial criteria are important in an acquisition review, they are no more important than subjective criteria. They are still important, however, and when a company sets a minimum anticipated rate of return that a candidate cannot satisfy, the candidate may be eliminated, but only after all other criteria are considered.

Rates of return and price/earnings multiples were common financial ratios used and were applied when an existing business was being acquired. Such ratios did not apply when the principal reason for the acquisition was to buy new technology, for example.

It is interesting that many said that they wanted to make as quick a determination as possible of the price range at which the business was for sale before providing an in-depth investigation of the acquisition. If they could not reach an agreement on the framework for a negotiation of price it was unlikely that they would proceed further. The more rigorous application of financial ratios and tests tended to take place during the detailed investigation after price range had been established. At this stage all companies performed a thorough review to compare historical and forecast financial results with predefined financial criteria. Most companies used price/earnings multiples and predefined rates of return to judge acquisition candidates. This information was then used to do a precise valuation of the candidate, to be used later in final negotiations of the purchase price.

The basis for ratios used was generally derived by comparison with other companies in the particular industry and with the actual performance of existing divisions or subsidiaries of the acquirer. Most companies prepared pro forma financial statements to determine what the combined operations would look like. Some companies used computerized financial models to perform this analysis.

J. *Are the accounting and financial reporting implications of the potential acquisition considered in the formulation of the financial acquisition criteria?*

In discussing the financial reporting considerations reviewed during the acquisition review process most companies, particularly since they are public, said they were concerned about how their consolidated performance would appear. Detrimental effects to the consolidated statements would be enough impetus to decide that the acquisition candidate was not appropriate. Such detrimental effects were uncovered when pro forma financial statements were prepared by the acquirer. The impact of the transaction on the financial statements of the acquirer was generally reviewed with the acquirer's auditors.

Acquisition Team

A. *How is the company organized to evaluate and consummate acquisitions?*

The rationale for posing this question was that we felt it would tell us whether the company has an acquisition team. We were aware that the companies we approached were active acquirers, and therefore probably had some sort of organized approach for undertaking acquisitions that would be useful to pass on to our readers. By the time we reached this question, we usually had an understanding of the company's organizational structure and, in particular, how it worked in the case of acquisitions.

Virtually all the companies we interviewed had organized themselves in a different manner to carry out their acquisition programs. In some cases the differences were subtle and in others they were major, but upon reflection we were able to classify the structures adopted by the companies interviewed as falling between two extremes.

At one end of the extreme were the companies that had an informal and ad hoc approach to evaluating and consummating acquisitions. In this approach the acquisition team was typically made up of the CEO and his senior officers. The company did not maintain a full-time acquisition department and usually drew on internal support staff to make various analyses as required. In all cases in which this approach was taken there tended to be a high level of personal interest by the CEO in participating actively in a hands-on way in the acquisition process and in particular in handling the negotiations. Whenever this approach was taken, the companies were successful acquirers. The reasons for their success are discussed in the report.

The other approach was to set up a full-time acquisition department, usually headed up by a vice president of corporate development. This department was responsible on an ongoing basis for uncovering acquisitions and reviewing candidates of interest. In many cases it was also responsible for conducting much of the negotiations. Most companies interviewed tended to be polarized at one end or the other.

It should be pointed out that even in the most highly structured approach, with a large and sophisticated full-time acquisition department, the corporate group did not in any way completely delegate the acquisition process to the acquisition department. In order for the company to be a successful acquirer, the corporate group (composed of the CEO and his senior officers) had to remain very active members of the acquisition team. In a couple of the companies with large corporate acquisition departments, we noticed that recent changes in the CEO indicated that the company's current priorities were unlikely to be focused on acquisitions. The acquisition departments were still actively pursuing potential acquisitions. However, in our view, it was highly unlikely that new candidates would be acquired.

In both cases the corporate group was involved in the highest level of decisions: in setting the broad acquisition criteria, as previously described; in deciding whether a candidate had the potential to warrant a more detailed review; and in negotiating and completing the deal.

The significant difference between these two approaches is that in the informal or less structured approach, the corporate group is certain to have the close involvement of the CEO. We found this involvement to be critical in enabling a company to make decisions about prospective acquisition candidates quickly and in providing the support and commitment necessary to maintain the momentum required to consummate transactions. Where the process was more highly structured, with a full-time acquisition department, it was critical for the CEO and senior officers to keep taking an active part in the acquisition process and to be closely involved in the key decisions to be made throughout.

B. *Who actually comprises the acquisition team?*

As discussed above, the heart of the acquisition team, whether the company has a full-time acquisition department or not, is the corporate group, and the driving force for successful acquirers is the CEO. In reviewing this question with those interviewed we focused on the support staff needed by the team to carry out the acquisition process.

Where the corporate group is the acquisition team, the senior officers of that group normally have functional experts in such areas as marketing, finance, and legal reporting to them. These experts, reporting to their vice president, are used to provide the input and analyses discussed and reviewed at the corporate group meetings. If necessary, outside specialists—real estate appraisers, for example—will be hired as required. Usually one of the senior officers will be given responsibility for pulling together the reviews of all those involved. Not infrequently this task falls to the vice president of finance.

When the company has a full-time acquisition department, this department is usually staffed with middle managers who are functional experts in fields such as marketing, finance, law, and engineering. As previously mentioned, this group was normally headed by the vice president of corporate development, who would then be responsible either to a corporate group of senior officers or directly to the CEO.

Having a small group of senior officers responsible for making acquisitions appeared to allow companies to target in rapidly on companies of interest, principally because the senior officers were the ultimate decision makers. With little support staff assistance, they appeared to be able to focus quickly on companies that would be of interest and reach a decision on whether to acquire or not. By their very highly structured nature the companies with full-time acquisition departments appeared to take longer to complete acquisitions. Some recognized this but accepted it as the price of being large.

C. *When is the acquisition team activated?*

    (i) Does the team undertake a detailed purchase investigation (basis for offer or confirmatory)?

In all acquisitions of private companies a detailed purchase investigation was conducted before buying. Where the companies initially entered into a nonbinding letter of intent, the detailed purchase investigation would be conducted to confirm the pricing indicated in the letter of intent and to provide the basis for drafting a detailed agreement of purchase and sale. The final agreement of purchase and sale frequently provides for a detailed audit of account balances to be done at or near the date of closing, with adjustments to be made in accordance with the terms of the agreement of purchase and sale.

Once again, whether the acquisition candidate was a public or a private company had a bearing on the situation. When the candidate was a public company, the acquisition team might analyze it and prepare an offer on the basis of publicly available information without ever contacting the candidate directly. Under these circumstances the purchase investigation would not be conducted until after the company had been acquired.

When the acquisition candidate was a private company, the investigation was conducted prior to making an offer. Although it is possible to come up with an approximate offer price that might be incorporated into a nonbinding letter of intent, most acquirers wanting to purchase private companies waited until the purchase investigation was complete before signing a binding agreement of purchase and sale.

It was interesting to find, particularly in the United States, that the completion of a purchase investigation was frequently augmented with an opinion from an investment banker on the fairness of the price being paid so that the board of directors could be satisfied that it had fulfilled its "due diligence" obligations. This use of an independent opinion has not been as predominant in Canada. The need for it in the United States appears to be a result of the extent to which courts have made directors of companies accountable to shareholders and investors.

(ii) Does the team undertake a thorough evaluation for specific purposes? (accounting, marketing, manufacturing, facilities, etc.)

The acquisition team, whether informally put together or including a full-time acquisition department, has or is given access to functional experts who analyze each particular function of the organization in question. The marketing, manufacturing, and other functional areas are examined in detail to ensure that all considerations are reviewed and factored into the final decision of whether or not to make an offer for the company.

D. *Who reviews and monitors the activities of the team?*

The CEO has overall responsibility for ensuring that his team is able to achieve the number and type of acquisitions he has set as his goal. This question was directed at identifying the principal individual in the corporate group who is charged with making sure that not only are all the tasks done but also that all the necessary discussions are held at the various discussion points in the process on a timely basis.

Where the corporate group is the acquisition team, one member of that group is generally designated as responsible for this coordination. The person so designated was frequently the vice president for finance, although the responsibility might change among members of the group, depending on the particular acquisition and the relative work loads and time commitments of its various members.

When the company had a full-time acquisition department, this responsibility fell to the vice president of corporate development.

Acquisition Search Methods

A. *To whom is information directed relating to acquisition candidates who are voluntarily brought to the company?*

The purpose of this question was to determine the document flow in the organization on a day-to-day basis. However, by the time we had reached this question in the interview process, we normally were aware of who would be responsible for reviewing acquisition candidates voluntarily brought to the company.

As previously described, exactly who would review acquisition candidates varied, depending on the type of organization structure for reviewing acquisition opportunities. Where the corporation had an acquisition department, the acquisition candidate would normally be given to someone in the department to make an initial assessment of whether the opportunity would be of any interest. Where there was no acquisition department, the candidate would be reviewed by one of the senior officers in the corporate group. The senior officer might even be the CEO who, after his initial determination of potential interest, would then pass along the opportunity for further review to the other members of the corporate group.

Where an organization was highly decentralized, a small acquisition opportunity would be reviewed at the divisional or subsidiary level. Only if it were an acquisition opportunity involving significant dollars would it then be passed up to the corporate group. Often acquisition opportunities were addressed to the CEO who, by spending only a few moments reviewing the situation, could determine quickly whether or not there would be any interest on his part. Conversely, when the acquisition opportunity was dealt with by the acquisition department, it would compare the opportunity with predetermined broad acquisition criteria to decide whether or not it was worthy of further consideration by the corporate group.

It was evident that when these opportunities were reviewed first by the acquisition department it took longer to respond with an indication of the level of interest. Some companies felt they may have lost some opportunities this way. Other companies solved the problem by having the vice president of corporate development review the opportunities first, so that he could, if any prospects looked of particular interest, see that they were dealt with on a priority basis.

B. *Does the company actively search out acquisition candidates which meet these criteria?*

All companies who were active acquirers undertook, in one form or another, to search out prospective acquisitions. We found, however, that there were two basic approaches—an active approach and a passive approach. Most companies used a combination of both approaches.

The passive approach generally relied on an extensive network of industry and financial community contacts to identify prospective acquisition opportunities. It appeared to us that this approach had become particularly effective in identifying opportunities for companies with a consistent history of making acquisitions. This reputation for making acquisitions meant that the entire financial community would consider them in determining a logical purchaser for businesses they knew might be up for sale.

The active search program normally included a thorough industry search for prospects likely to meet the company's acquisition criteria. This active approach to searching for acquisition candidates was found to be predominant where an acquisition department existed. However, where a corporate group of senior officers was responsible for handling all acquisition opportunities, the group would sometimes carry out a search when it had a specific acquisition interest it wished fulfilled in a certain time frame. Companies without a full-time acquisition department were more likely to rely on opportunities being presented to them through their extensive industry contacts, investment dealer contacts, bankers, brokers, or others who might be familiar with their acquisition interests. Where companies undertook an extensive and ongoing active search program, they also relied extensively on the contacts of the corporate group and board of directors.

It was evident that the active approach uncovered more prospects than were presented to companies following only the passive approach, but it did not appear to us that it necessarily resulted in more transactions. This may be because a lot of the "opportunities" identified under the more active search program were not really for sale.

An important finding was that companies that followed what we describe as the passive approach to carrying out acquisition searches made their interest in acquisitions very well known within the industry in which they operated and to the financial community, to ensure that acquisition opportunities were presented to them on an ongoing basis. Furthermore, most companies using this approach would evaluate the opportunity within a matter of days or even hours and give a quick reply as to their level of interest.

Companies following the passive approach exclusively felt that the ability to respond quickly and not waste the time of those presenting opportunities ensured that their contacts would keep them high on their list of companies to be approached with opportunities.

C. *If so, who is responsible for undertaking searches?*

Where an acquisition department existed this department would carry out the active search process. Where companies without an acquisition department undertook an active search program, one of the senior officers of that group would have certain staff made available to him who would assist in carrying out the organized search process.

In the case of successful acquirers it appears that all members of the corporate group are expected to maintain contacts that will lead to the identification of opportunities to make acquisitions.

D. *Does the company use "outsiders" to assist in its search program?*

The use of outsiders to carry out a search program was found to be more usual in companies that did not have their own acquisition departments. Where an acquisition department was an integral part of the organization, hiring outsiders to carry out a search did not make economic or managerial sense. However, when management expertise was not available to carry out a search or management did not want to devote the time required to carry out the search, outsiders might be used.

Furthermore, particularly in the United States, where it was quite common to have an investment banker actively involved in the acquisition process, these bankers would normally carry out an acquisition search for little or no charge since they were frequently working, at least in part, on a commission basis. Since these investment bankers would end up being involved in the transaction at some stage and would still reap the same level of fees, there was certain economic sense in having them involved up front and performing as much work as possible in identifying acquisition opportunities.

Certain companies were specifically against having third parties assist them in carrying out acquisition searches, as they were concerned about disclosing their strategic plan to outsiders.

All companies interviewed were familiar with the recent increases in available data bases of extensive listings of companies that can be used in making acquisition searches. Ease of access to these data bases from in-house computer systems or time-sharing with outside facilities improved the ability of companies to carry out their own acquisition search.

E. *How are acquisition candidates voluntarily presented to the company reviewed?*

Normally, where a small group of senior corporate officers is involved in the acquisition process, particularly when the CEO is actively involved, the CEO may review acquisition opportunities initially to determine if there is any interest and if there is, pass them on to the remainder of the group for a more thorough review. As previously discussed, when an acquisition department is in place, all acquisition opportunities, unless identified by a member of the corporate group, are usually forwarded to that department. We did not find that the treatment of acquisition candidates voluntarily presented to the company was any different from that given to acquisition candidates the company actively sought out on its own. Furthermore, most companies using either type of approach tried to have a policy on the timing of the review process for new opportunities to ensure a quick response to interested acquisition candidates. Such timeliness normally included getting back within a couple of weeks or, at maximum, within a month to inform the candidate of potential interest. Typically, when the CEO was actively involved in the acquisition process, a response could be given almost immediately.

F. *Who determines which candidates should be seriously pursued?*

As previously described, when the CEO was actively involved in the acquisition process, he would frequently make the decision as to whether or not an acquisition candidate should be pursued seriously. When an acquisition department was in place, the vice president in charge of that department would make a recommendation to the CEO regarding whether or not to pursue an opportunity, but it would be the CEO who would decide whether or not to proceed.

Acquisitions in Foreign Jurisdictions

A. *Is the process by which the company searches, evaluates, negotiates, and finances the acquisition, as presented to us today, different when the company is pursuing an acquisition in a foreign jurisdiction?*

Although information was desired on the company's experience in undertaking acquisitions in foreign jurisdictions, little detailed information on this topic was obtained. Most of the companies interviewed had not undertaken acquisitions outside of North America and mentioned no significant differences apart from specific regulatory requirements between Canada and the United States. Those that had expanded outside of North America did not feel that they had followed a different approach, but noted that the specific expertise of lawyers and accountants familiar with the country typically was required to solve technical problems.

In foreign acquisitions one major problem highlighted was the repatriation of earnings. To solve this problem some companies expand abroad to use funds that cannot otherwise be repatriated.

Many companies interviewed felt that North America offered them enough opportunities for expansion and pointed out that acquisitions close to home were much easier to monitor. As well, some companies mentioned countries in which they would not invest. Typically these were in politically sensitive areas of the world.

Specific differences in conducting searches, evaluations, and negotiations and in financing foreign acquisitions were not noted.

Evaluation of Acquisition Candidates

A. *What information and commitments does the company require from the acquisition candidate before proceeding to a detailed evaluation?*

Because performing a detailed evaluation of an acquisition candidate can be a time-consuming and costly process, we sought to uncover the sort of commitments from the candidate that companies require, or information about the candidate they must have before they will commit themselves to an evaluation. The answer to this question differed, depending on whether the companies were acquiring private or public companies.

Where a public company was to be acquired, extensive information generally was available from public sources, including SEC filings in the United States. In some cases this information base might be satisfactory to determine an offer price and no actual commitment or passage of information from the candidate was required prior to performing a detailed evaluation. In this situation, it was more typical for the detailed evaluation to be made without contacting the acquisition prospect.

When the company was anticipating a hostile takeover, no commitment was required of the acquisition candidate. When a friendly takeover was being considered, the management of the prospective acquirer normally would contact the management and major shareholder of the acquisition candidate to obtain an understanding that they both would be working toward a common goal. We found that the unsolicited public takeover represented the extreme case, where no prior contact was made with the company before making an offer.

The private company represents the other extreme. Here, access to detailed information from the company and its shareholders is almost always required before a final decision can be made that the company is of real interest to the purchaser. We found that there were various levels of evaluation and investigation undertaken of prospective acquisition candidates. There were also various levels of commitment that most companies wanted from prospective candidates at each level of evaluation. These various levels of commitment and evaluation were designed to answer the following questions:

1. Is the company of interest, and, if so, is it likely to be available at a reasonable price?

2. Is the company of sufficient interest to undertake a detailed purchase investigation and can the basis of a deal be agreed upon?

3. Does the detailed purchase investigation justify making a firm offer of purchase and sale?

Question 1. Is the company of interest and, if so, is it likely to be available at a reasonable price?

Where the prospective candidate has been identified as a result of the purchaser's own search it is usual for the purchaser not to know whether the owners are prepared to sell. In these circumstances we found that acquirers liked to contact the acquisition candidate as soon as a decision was made that the prospect met the acquirer's broad criteria and the prospect was therefore an acquisition candidate. The willingness to sell can be determined to a large extent by the cooperation of the prospect in providing additional information to enable the purchaser to satisfy itself that it has a definite interest in seriously pursuing an acquisition. Most companies recognized, however, that many owners of private companies are curious about the potential value of their company, so the mere willingness to provide information does not necessarily indicate that the company is seriously for sale.

At the time of the initial contact most prospective purchasers spend considerable time with the owner to understand his personal situation and to discuss with him his view of the value of the business and approach to determining that value. This is necessary to make a judgment as to whether there is likely to be a basis on which a deal can be made. Most purchasers did not like to spend a great deal of time investigating an acquisition without first knowing that there was a realistic opportunity for a sale.

The exact type of information each acquirer expects to receive initially from an acquisition candidate was not specifically outlined to us but, from the general discussions we had, we found that it ranged from detailed financial information, product line information, performance records, and market analyses, to very limited financial information.

Where the owners of the business were independent of management, most acquirers also wanted to determine that the management of the company would be receptive to a change of ownership.

Question 2. Is the company of sufficient interest to undertake a detailed purchase investigation and can the basis of a deal be agreed upon?

Most acquirers liked to reach the answer to this question as soon as possible after receiving enough information from the acquisition candidate to establish whether they have a definite interest in acquiring the business. Many indicated that they liked to get the candidate to sign a nonbinding letter of intent that detailed the basis of a deal. This was designed to confirm further the seriousness of the intention to sell the prospect's business before proceeding to a detailed purchase investigation.

Question 3. Does the detailed purchase investigation justify making a firm offer of purchase and sale?

The purchase investigation is a detailed audit to confirm for the purchaser the reliability of the financial and other information provided and is intended to establish a level of comfort with respect to the prospects for the business. Further negotiations will take place between the parties based on the information obtained during the review. The principal focus of the review is to establish a final price for the purpose of signing a binding agreement of purchase and sale.

In the agreement of purchase and sale a number of items such as final balances of inventory accounts will be subject to audit at the date of closing. These final audits, of the date of closing account balances, are generally considered to be part of the overall purchase investigation.

B. *How is the company organized to conduct an in-depth analysis?*

This again depended largely on whether or not the company had a full-time acquisition department. Where such a department was in place the review was conducted by members of that department. Where no acquisition department existed a review team was generally put together on an ad hoc basis, composed of various members of the corporate group and functional experts from within and without the company.

C. *Who conducts the in-depth analysis?*

Where an acquisition department existed it would normally constitute the review team and would supplement its review by functional specialists from outside the company where necessary. Where no acquisition department existed it would normally be the responsibility of the corporate group of senior officers to coordinate a task force to undertake a thorough review of a candidate's operations. The members of that task force would be drawn from the various functional areas of the company or its subsidiaries. Included in the team of people who performs the evaluation would be one or more individuals proficient in analyzing and valuing businesses. Normally the members of the team each had a particular functional specialty, such as marketing, law, finance, or technology.

During the evaluation it is frequently necessary for a company to call upon specialists to perform specific reviews. Examples of outsiders included accountants, lawyers, tax specialists, appraisers, and engineers. Even when an acquisition department existed, it was not uncommon for it to call on experts within its own organization from various subsidiaries or divisions to assist in undertaking the review.

D. *Who has the overall responsibility for the analysis?*

As was previously described, who had overall responsibility for the analysis depended on the organizational structure of the company for making acquisitions. Where the company had a full-time acquisition department the vice president of corporate development would have overall responsibility for conducting the detailed analysis. Where no acquisition department existed one of the vice presidents in the corporate group would be given overall responsibility for the analysis or, if each vice president was responsible for a particular area of the analysis, for coordinating their input and the work of any other support staff used in the review.

Frequently this responsibility was given to the vice president of finance. He was probably chosen as the most logical person because of the financial skills that are necessary to establish a value for the business to be acquired. In many cases, however, overall responsibility would be allocated to alternate members of the corporate group, depending on the type of acquisition and the relative work loads.

E. *Is the evaluation conducted in such a manner as to identify in priority whether the candidate meets the most critical criteria?*

Because of the apparent importance of acquisition criteria, we asked this question to determine how acquisition criteria are used during the evaluation process. In the initial review leading up to the preparation of a letter of intent, the emphasis of the review was on determining that the prospect could satisfy the most important of the acquirer's criteria. However, once acquirers got beyond the letter of intent into the detailed purchase investigation, most of them tended to complete the detailed purchase investigation before standing back and checking that, overall, the prospect still substantially met the criteria. Thus unless specific and obvious problems were encountered by the acquisition review team at this stage, the evaluation would be continued until completed before a final decision was made. It would be expected that any of the problems could be dealt with by adjusting the initial purchase price outlined in the letter of intent.

F. *Who reviews the ongoing results of the evaluation and decides whether or not to continue?*

During the various stages of the evaluation, which is a time-consuming and costly undertaking for acquirers, we thought it was worth discussing whether the process was monitored on an ongoing basis so that it could be stopped at any time that the candidate was seen as failing to meet an important criterion. It was found that such monitoring actually is done through close supervision by the person with overall responsibility for the analysis—usually the vice president of corporate development or the vice president of finance.

Furthermore, since the evaluation is carried out by fairly senior middle managers and senior officers of the company, they all had access to those people within the organization who could inform them whether or not a specific factor identified in the review was critical enough to warrant being brought to the immediate attention of the vice president in charge of the review.

G. *How is the information collected and communicated to those responsible for making the final acquisition decision?*

There tended to be a high level of both formal and informal communication throughout the review process. Where the acquisition review was carried out by a small group of corporate officers with the close involvement of the CEO, the information would be communicated on almost a daily basis at times to the members of the group as they interacted on a regular basis. This constant communication would on occasion be supported by documentation prepared by support staff, such as copies of financial statements from the vice president of finance or copies of a marketing study from the vice president of marketing.

In contrast, where the acquisition process was carried out in a formalized manner, with an acquisition department performing the review, this department would normally complete its review and provide a very detailed report to the vice president responsible for the team. This vice president would then compile a more summarized report for presentation to senior management and ultimately to the CEO for presentation to the board of directors.

A fundamental difference between the two approaches appeared to be that when the complete report was prepared for presentation to senior officers, more time was normally required for its preparation; thus more time could be required until the CEO decided how the candidate should be treated. In contrast, when the CEO was an integral part of the corporate group reviewing acquisition opportunities, decisions were generally made quickly and decisively.

A number of the companies interviewed stated that because of the emergence of "due diligence" in the United States, they made sure that a thorough evaluation was always conducted of acquisition candidates. In the United States the ready availability of legal counsel for class-action suits has led shareholders to consider suing management and directors of corporations if they do not agree with a particular acquisition decision. Therefore, CEOs, officers, and directors must ensure that full documentation of their decisions is available in order to prove their "due diligence" to the public. As a result of this requirement, most acquirers do written reports to ensure that they have satisfied their public duty.

In the United States, particularly on transactions that were of significant size relative to the purchaser, comfort opinions were usually sought from investment bankers as to the reasonableness of the price being paid.

H. *How are the results of the evaluation utilized to assist in negotiations?*

Since much time and effort were incurred in carrying out the evaluation of acquisition candidates, we decided to ask how the information obtained in the course of the review was used in the negotiation process. Clearly, if useful information were found during the evaluation process, it would be valuable in conducting the negotiations. We found that information collected through the evaluation process was transmitted to the senior officers carrying out the negotiations in a way that enabled them to use such information during negotiation sessions. The information was, in fact, critical to the negotiations. Where the CEO was a member of the corporate group carrying out the acquisition review and was familiar on a day-to-day basis with the progress of the review, he was familiar with all items that could be helpful to him in the ultimate negotiations.

When the CEO was removed from the acquisition review process, this information would be specifically highlighted in a report to him. Also, usually the CEO and the vice president of corporate development in charge of the acquisition review were in close communication. This process worked fine in certain organizations, but the CEO had to rely heavily on the vice president of corporate development to make him aware of items of relevance and importance to the negotiation process.

More typically it was found that all levels of the evaluation were performed prior to or in the course of actual negotiation sessions and almost always produced information essential to or useful in the negotiations.

I. *In the course of making the financial evaluation:*
   (i) Are the accounting and financial reporting implications of the acquisition fully evaluated?

In the actual interview sessions the responses to this question were very similar to those obtained under the question relating to financial acquisition criteria. Although it was recognized at the outset of the interview process that this question would have certain similarities to that posed under financial acquisition criteria, we decided to ask it separately to try and obtain more information on the importance and relevance of accounting and financial reporting information to the acquisition process.

We found that, as previously stated, financial and accounting implications were reviewed thoroughly during the evaluation process. With respect to these matters, the senior officers interviewed felt that the most critical factor was the effect the acquisition would have on the consolidated publicly disclosed information. Usually the company's auditors were asked to assist in assessing the impact the acquisition might have on the company's reported financial position and operating results, with a particular emphasis on earnings per share.

(ii) Is the current financial information of the candidate examined to determine the underlying value of the company?

Using what technique?

The responses to this question were fairly general. However, most of them were similar to those previously outlined under the financial criteria question. We found that the ultimate purpose of the review was to arrive at or justify a valuation of the acquisition candidate. The approach taken to arriving at a valuation differed, depending on the specific industry in which the acquisition candidate operated. In all cases someone proficient in the art of valuation—either an independent third-party valuator or an internal expert—was called upon to review the candidate to establish the appropriate valuation approach and to arrive at a valuation. Valuation approaches mentioned include the use of discounted cash flows, capitalization of expected earnings, and an asset valuation. A replacement cost approach often was used when the main purpose of the acquisition was, for example, to acquire new technology. In that case value was determined more by comparing the acquirer's estimated cost of duplicating the technology with the cost of acquiring it through an acquisition.

When the valuation was done, acquisition candidates were often compared with subsidiaries or divisions within the acquirer's company that had similar operations. The acquirer also compared the evaluation process needed with other transactions it knew about—including those used in prior acquisitions—in order to establish the most appropriate valuation approach to be used.

At what stage in the acquisition process?

We found that the valuation of an acquisition candidate initially was performed on a conceptual basis during the review of the broad acquisition criteria. The reason for the computation was that it was normally one of the acquisition criteria used to determine whether or not the candidate was within the financial capability of the acquirer. It was also essential to establish the basic approach to valuation early, so that in the initial discussions it could be determined whether or not a mutual approach to value was likely to be agreed upon by both parties. This was necessary to determine that there was a reasonable expectation of eventually completing the deal.

In the second level of review leading up to the letter of intent the approach to and calculation of value would be refined.

On completion of the detailed purchase investigation, the information obtained from the review would be assessed in light of the basis used in determining value in the letter of intent. It was usually hoped that adjustments to the purchase price could be used to settle any items of concern that were identified in the purchase investigation.

This differed when the acquisition candidate was a public company and an unsolicited offer was to be made. Under these circumstances a detailed valuation would probably have to be performed on the basis of publicly available information.

In most purchases of private companies it was recognized that the valuation might not be as precise as desired; therefore, in the actual purchase and sale agreement there might be contingency or price adjustment clauses providing that should certain assumptions not turn out as expected, the purchase price would be adjusted accordingly.

In the public company valuation, based on publicly available information, the offer usually could not be made on a contingency basis. Therefore, the initial offer given would have to be that at which the acquirer was willing to transact. Under these circumstances, the initial valuation would be made on a fairly thorough basis to ensure that all matters had been considered when the offer price was finally fixed.

(iii) In evaluating a candidate are the tax implications of the transaction to the purchaser and vendor reviewed in detail?

We found that the tax implications were reviewed by both the acquirer and the acquisition candidate to ensure that the best tax structure for the contemplated transaction was identified for both parties. This review was performed by either internal tax specialists of the company or independent third parties (legal and accounting). We were told that the acquirer frequently tried to structure the deal in the most advantageous tax manner for the candidate in order to show good faith and to provide the candidate with the best purchase price possible under the circumstances.

Certain of the companies interviewed were proud of their tax expertise and had used such expertise in order to effect transactions at prices they thought were below true market value.

Negotiations and the Final Decision

A. *Who reviews the results of the evaluations and decides to go on to negotiations?*

We found that no matter how the organization was structured to carry out its acquisition program (that is, whether or not it had a full-time acquisition department), the corporate group of senior officers or the CEO normally determined whether or not the company should proceed to negotiations.

In contrast, where the corporate group is not actively involved in the acquisition review itself, it is normally presented with a lengthy report outlining the recommendation of the acquisition team and uses this report to determine if it should proceed to negotiations. If authority is vested in the corporate group, it makes the decision to move on to negotiations without the approval of the CEO. In this instance, if the deal is agreed upon, it is subject to the approval of the CEO and the board of directors.

Where the acquisition was small by the company's own standards, it was possible for a division- or subsidiary-level president to determine that the company would proceed to negotiations, recognizing that no deal would be finalized without corporate level and possibly board approval.

B. *Who sets the general framework of the terms and conditions under which the negotiations are to be undertaken?*

Since the terms and conditions under which negotiations are carried out appeared to be critical to making a successful acquisition, we hoped this question might provide some insights into the negotiation phase. However, though an understanding of the information flow within the organization was obtained, we did not have the time to obtain detailed insights into the actual setting of terms and conditions of the negotiation process.

We found that in all cases the corporate group, including the CEO, determines the terms and conditions under which negotiations are undertaken.

C. Who actually conducts the negotiations?

For a major transaction, the CEO had to be directly involved in negotiations in order to ensure that the acquisition candidate felt it was being given proper attention by the acquirer. However, except for the largest transactions, negotiations are often conducted by members of the corporate group relying on the CEO for support and involvement when issues have to be approved in order for negotiations to proceed.

When the company did not have an acquisition department, the CEO was often extensively involved in the negotiations. The CEO's enthusiasm and interest in conducting acquisitions was particularly evident in such a company. When the company had a full-time acquisition department, the vice president of corporate development would be heavily involved in carrying out negotiations, subject to the approval of the CEO. We were told that in order for those involved to carry on successful negotiations, some companies have prior role-playing of the negotiation process to ensure that the negotiations run smoothly. Such role-playing could include one vice president taking the position of the vendor.

Where an acquisition candidate would become part of an existing division or subsidiary of the acquirer, it was usual for the president of the respective division or subsidiary to be involved in the negotiations. The reason for such involvement was to ensure that the president was satisfied that the candidate met his own criteria and that he was truly interested in and committed to a merger of the new operation with his own.

D. Who approves the results of the negotiations and finalizes the deal?

It was not surprising to find the results of the negotiations were always approved by the CEO whether or not he was directly involved in the negotiations himself. The deal was frequently made final by the CEO with the help of other senior officers, but was subject to the approval of the board of directors.

In order for the company to transact quickly, most corporations have an executive committee of the board of directors consisting of a small group of directors who can apprise the CEO on the likelihood of the board of directors approving the contemplated acquisition.

E. *At what point in the acquisition process is initial determination of an acceptable purchase price made?*

This question was actually answered during the questions on valuation of the acquisition candidate. As previously described, during the evaluation process a valuation of the acquisition candidate is carried out at various levels of the acquisition review. The review is designed to provide the acquirer with an early determination of an acceptable purchase price that is refined later, when the report based on the detailed review is completed.

F. *How does the company maintain the initiative to keep up the momentum in the course of negotiations?*

In order for a company to be a successful acquirer, it was important for it to maintain the momentum of negotiations; that would improve the chances of completing a deal. During our discussions we were given various suggestions on how to maintain the momentum of negotiations. Each of the people interviewed thought that his suggestions were a critical element of being a successful acquirer.

Since the suggestions on how to maintain the momentum of negotiations are of such importance, each one outlined to us is provided in the summary of findings and conclusions in Chapter 3 of the report.

G. *At what point in the acquisition process is an attempt made to reach an agreement in principle with the vendor before proceeding further with an evaluation or negotiations?*

In posing this question we wished to understand when in the acquisition process an agreement in principle was reached with the acquisition candidate before the company would proceed with an evaluation or be prepared to enter negotiations. The reason for obtaining an agreement in principle was not only so that the acquirer could obtain more information about the candidate, but also to enable the acquirer to determine if there was a reasonable prospect of consummating a deal at a fair price. As stated previously, acquirers did not have to invest too much time and effort in reviewing and negotiating with the candidate without this assurance.

In private company acquisitions a verbal agreement in principle is often effected early in the acquisition process, normally concurrent with the request by the prospective acquirer to obtain more detailed information. The verbal agreement or understanding might then be converted into a nonbinding letter of intent issued prior to commencing a detailed purchase investigation. This practice is not followed by all companies, but it was the most common approach followed for private company acquisitions.

Financing the Acquisition

A. *Does the company have a preference in the method it uses to finance acquisitions, and why?*

Since it was anticipated that the majority of our readers—particularly members of the Association and the Society—would be financially oriented people, we tried to get more detail on how acquisitions are financed. From the responses obtained, it was difficult to generalize the preferences of acquirers in the method of financing acquisitions. Most acquirers sought the best financing technique that was appropriate in the particular circumstance and in the economic environment at the time the acquisition was being made. However, certain preferences were noted:

- Cash and bank loans were used wherever possible, to avoid any dilution of equity.
- Shares were used, provided no material dilution occurred.
- Leveraged buy-outs were also popular.

There was a common attitude of remaining flexible and being prepared to deal with shares, cash, or debt, whichever would also best meet the vendor's needs.

Although the preferences outlined above are very general, they serve to highlight the overall position of most of those interviewed, which is to try to leave the vendor in a flexible position so that he may feel he is obtaining the best financial structure and tax position available. The only strong preference noted in our discussions was for using debt and common cash rather than shares. This preference seemed to relate to the acquirer's stock market performance at the date of the transaction relative to the company's underlying asset value. Where the stock market was placing a high premium on the company's shares so that an acquisition could be transacted without materially diluting the acquirer's earnings per share, most companies would consider using shares. Otherwise, the use of shares was rarely considered unless a major reorganization through merger or combination was being considered.

B. *Who recommends the financing package that will be used and who approves it?*

We posed this question to determine who within the corporate structure recommends the financing package. In all cases the chief financial officer recommended the financing package. His decision is normally based upon analyses made by his staff and, where necessary, by outside tax and legal advisors.

Occasionally the CEO may be quite knowledgable in structuring acquisitions; in that case he would have significant input into structuring the financial package. Normally when that happened the CEO had had a financial background and often had been the vice president of finance.

Every effort is made to recommend a financial structure that is as simplistic as possible. Also, the availability of financing for acquisition was generally arranged early, in the initial stages of establishing an active acquisition program.

C. *Do you perceive any changes in the financial techniques to be used for acquisitions in the future?*

Though the questionnaire was geared toward obtaining information on the acquisition process, we thought it would be useful to obtain the views of those interviewed on whether they anticipate changes in financial techniques to be used for acquisitions in the future. The responses we obtained were fairly general and not that enlightening. The preference for cash and debt has already been noted, as well as the fact that the performance of the company's stock determined whether or not they would consider issuing shares. A number of those interviewed said that in the future they could foresee a greater use of joint ventures to bring more financial capability and management expertise to a given project.

Most of those interviewed thought that cash-rich companies would continue to make acquisitions by cash and that they would avoid issuing shares so as not to dilute their shareholders' interest. Others stated that they were not frightened to dilute their equity, and they felt that if their shares were trading at a reasonable price they would use them to make acquisitions.

During the course of our interviews, interest rates were at an all-time high; as a result, most of those companies interviewed stated that they thought it would be extremely difficult for companies to carry out leveraged buy-outs. However, they thought that in the future this technique would be continued where companies had low financing costs or where the availability of funds improved because of declining interest rates.

Review of the Company's Acquisition Activities

A. *At what point in the acquisition process are plans made for assimilation?*

Many of those interviewed considered the planning for assimilation an important part of the acquisition process. However, the answers to this question varied widely. The amount of time and effort spent on an assimilation plan depended to a large extent on whether the company operated on a decentralized or a centralized basis and whether the candidate was to be operated independently, with its own management, or was to be integrated with an existing business unit of the acquirer. When the acquisition candidate was to operate on a decentralized basis and not integrated into an existing business unit of the acquirer, little assimilation was necessary. Conversely, when the acquirer operated on a centralized basis and/or the candidate was to be integrated into an existing operating subsidiary or division, extensive assimilation planning had to be done.

Although all companies interviewed recognized that attention had to be paid to planning the assimilation of an acquisition candidate, most felt that they had not prepared such assimilation plans properly and on a timely basis in the past. Some companies indicated that serious thought to the problems of assimilation should be given at the outset of the process and others had prepared a detailed assimilation plan upon their initial review of an acquisition candidate.

Normally, once the acquisition was consummated, an integration team would be formed. The purpose of this integration team was to ensure that a proper plan for assimilation existed and that all problems were identified and resolved as soon as possible. Most companies, however, felt that they should have considered establishing such an integration team midway through the acquisition process, probably during the evaluation stage. The team could then be used to point up practical difficulties in consummating the transaction at an early date.

B. *To what does the company attribute its success in consummating acquisitions?*

Throughout this report we defined a successful acquirer as one that was able to close transactions. Although in our interviews we sought to understand the acquisition process and methods used to ensure successful acquisitions, was asked specifically if the interviewees had recommendations that they felt would assist in making acquisitions. In virtually all cases those interviewed had rather interesting ideas of why they were able to close deals for acquisitions and considered themselves successful acquirers. These specific findings are included in Chapter 3 of the report.

Reflections on the Past and Future

A. *Has the company changed its approach to making acquisitions, and if so, why?*

In trying to determine the acquisition process followed by companies, we asked if their approach to making acquisitions had changed. If it had, we wanted to know why. Most companies had an acquisition process in place and were satisfied with their process. Those that were in the process of changing or would consider changing their acquisition process were companies that had recently become active acquirers. They were still creating a suitable acquisition decision-making process for their own operations. Otherwise, a change in the acquisition process probably reflected some change in corporate strategies, either to a more active or to a less active acquisition program.

B. *Do you think that the company's approach to acquisitions in the future is likely to change, and if so, how and why?*

Question A above dealt with whether the company had actually changed its acquisition program in the past; this question deals with whether it anticipates changing its acquisition program in the future. As mentioned above, for both historical and prospective changes, the only reason found was a change in corporate strategies, resulting in a change in attitude of the corporation toward acquisitions. When such change warranted an improvement or scaling down of the acquisition process, this would be reflected in a change in the overall process.

C. *Does the company do a postacquisition review to determine how closely the business has conformed to its overall assessment at the time of purchase?*

In the normative literature, postacquisition review is considered to be outside the scope of the acquisition process. Most of the people we interviewed considered a postacquisition review to be part of the acquisition process, but they then admitted that they had not spent the time and effort to prepare such reviews properly in the past. Some companies interviewed did prepare these reviews, but the majority did not. This majority felt that it could probably have learned ways of improving its acquisition process if it had performed thorough postacquisition reviews of the companies it had acquired.

Bibliography

Articles

Alberts, William W. and James M. McTaggart, "The Divestiture Decision: An Introduction," *Mergers and Acquisitions*, Vol. 14, Fall 1979, pp. 18–30.

Baker, H. Kent, Thomas O. Miller, and Brian J. Ramsperger, "An Inside Look at Corporate Mergers and Acquisitions," *MSU Business Topics*, Vol. 29, Winter 1981, pp. 49–57.

Bergeron, Pierre G., "Strategy for Buying an Ongoing Business," *CA Magazine*, Vol. 108, May 1976, pp. 35–42.

Berolzheimer, Michael G., "Parting With Your 'Baby': One Man's Experience," *Harvard Business Review*, January–February 1980, pp. 6–11.

Buckley, Adrian A., "Some Guidelines for Acquisitions," *Accounting and Business Research*, Vol. 1, Summer 1971, pp. 215–232.

Catty, James P., "Canada's Most Significant Merger," *CA Magazine*, Vol. 116, September 1983, pp. 48–51.

Chakravarty, Subrata N., "Why Some Mergers Work and Many More Don't: An Interview With Peter Drucker," *Forbes*, Vol. 129, January 18, 1982, pp. 34–36.

Denholm, Donald H., "Acquisitions and the Management Accountant," *Management Accounting* (NAA), Vol. 50, December 1968, pp. 15–19.

Duhaime, Irene M. and G. Richard Patton, "Selling Off," *The Wharton Magazine*, Vol. 4, Winter 1980, pp. 43–47.

Gill, John and Ian Foulder, "Managing a Merger: The Acquisition and The Aftermath," *Personnel Management*, Vol. 10, January 1978, pp. 14–17.

Goldenberg, Susan, "Corporate Giants Spend Big to Diversify," *Financial Times of Canada*, December 4, 1978, p. 2.

Gormley, R. James, "Professional Risks in Purchase Audits and Reviews," *Journal of Accounting, Auditing and Finance*, Vol. 3, Summer 1980, pp. 293-312.

"The Great Takeover Binge," *Business Week*, November 1, 1977, pp. 176-184.

Grimm, W.T. & Co., 1978 to 1981 "Merger Summaries," published quarterly.

Herrmann, Arthur L., "A Decision Model for Mergers and Acquisitions," *Mergers and Acqusitions*, Spring 1976, pp. 14-21.

Malek, Fred V. and Gary E. MacDougal, "Master Plan for Merger Negotiations," *Harvard Business Review*, Vol. 48, January–February 1970, pp. 71-82.

Meadows, Edward, "Directory-Deals of the Year," *Fortune*, Vol. 105, January 25, 1982, pp. 36-40.

Mergers and Corporate Policy, published weekly, Cambridge Corp., Ipswich, Massachusetts, 1979, 1983.

Mintzberg, Henry, "Patterns in Strategy Formation," *International Studies of Management and Organization*, Vol. 9, no. 3, 1979, pp. 67-86.

Rappaport, Alfred, "Do You Know the Value of Your Company?" *Mergers and Acquisitions*, Vol. 14, Spring 1979, pp. 12-17.

Rhys, David Garel, "Anatomy of a Merger," *Accounting and Business Research*, no. 5, Winter 1972, pp. 46-52.

Rockwell, Willard F., Jr., "How to Acquire a Company," *Harvard Business Review*, Vol. 46, September–October 1968, pp. 121-132.

Salter, Malcolm S. and Wolf A. Weinhold, "Diversification via Acquisition: Creating Value," *Harvard Business Review*, July–August 1978, pp. 166-176.

Schlig, Joseph, "How to Acquire a Company," *Management World*, December 1980, pp. 27-29.

Spitalnic, Robert, "Financing the Acquisition: An Overview," *Management Guide to Mergers and Acquisitions*, John L. Harvey and Albert Newgarden (Eds.), Wiley-Interscience, New York, 1969.

Steyer, Robert, "Directory-Deals of the Year," *Fortune*, January 24, 1983, pp. 48-52.

Wallner, Nicholas, "Leveraged Buyouts: A Review of the State of the Art, Part I," *Mergers and Acquisitions*, Vol. 14, Fall 1979, pp. 4-13.

Wallner, Nicholas, "Leveraged Buyouts: A Review of the State of the Art, Part II," *Mergers and Acquisitions*, Vol. 14, Winter 1980, pp. 16-25.

Books

Bing, Gordon. *Corporate Acquisitions*, Gulf Publishing Co., Houston, Texas, 1980.

Bing, Gordon. *Corporate Divestment*, Gulf Publishing Co., Houston, Texas, 1978.

Campbell, Ian R. *The Principles and Practices of Business Valuation*, Richard De Boo Ltd., Toronto, Ontario, Canada, 1975.

Gordon, Lawrence A., Danny Miller, and Henry Mintzberg. *Normative Models in Managerial Decision-Making*, National Association of Accountants, New York, and The Society of Management Accountants of Canada, Hamilton, Ontario, Canada, 1975.

Jurek, Walter. *Directory of Acquisitions—1981*, Quality Services Co., Santa Barbara, California, 1982.

Jurek, Walter. *Merger and Acquisition Sourcebook—1983*, Quality Services Co., Santa Barbara, California, 1983.

Lee, Steven James and Robert Douglas Colman (Eds.). *Handbook of Mergers, Acquisitions and Buyouts*, Prentice-Hall, Inc., Englewood Cliffs, New Jersey, 1981.

McQuillan, Peter. *Financing Corporate Acquisitions*, Butterworths & Co. (Canada) Ltd., Toronto, Ontario, Canada, 1978.

Mergers and Corporate Policy, Yearbook on Corporate Mergers, Joint Ventures and Corporate Policy, 1980, 1982, 1983, Cambridge Corp., Ipswich, Massachusetts, 1981, 1982, 1983.

Newman, Peter C. *The Canadian Establishment, Vol. 1*, McLelland & Stewart, Toronto, Ontario, Canada, 1975.

Newman, Peter C. *The Canadian Establishment, Vol. II, The Acquisitors*, McLelland & Stewart, Toronto, Ontario, Canada, 1981.

Norin, Desmond B. and Warren Chippindale. *Acquisitions and Mergers in Canada, 2nd ed.*, Methuen, Toronto, Ontario, Canada, 1977.

Parsons, R.Q. and J.S. Baumgartner. *Anatomy of a Merger*, Prentice-Hall, Inc., Englewood Cliffs, New Jersey, 1970.

Peters, Thomas J. and Robert H. Waterman, Jr. *In Search of Excellence: Lessons from America's Best-Run Companies*, Harper & Row, New York, 1982.

Phalon, Richard. *The Takeover Barons of Wall Street*, G.P. Putnam's Sons, New York, 1981.

Scharf, Charles A. *Acquisitions, Mergers, Sales and Takeovers: A Handbook with Forms*, Prentice-Hall, Inc., Englewood Cliffs, New Jersey, 1971.